Editor

Mary S. Jones, M.A.

Editor in Chief

Karen J. Goldfluss, M.S. Ed.

Cover Artist

Tony Carrillo

Imaging

James Edward Grace

Craig Gunnell

Rosa C. See

Publisher

Mary D. Smith, M.S. Ed.

Author

Robert W. Smith

Correlations to the Common Core State Standards can be found at *http://www.teachercreated.com/standards/*.

The classroom teacher may reproduce the materials in this book and/or CD for use in a single classroom only. The reproduction of any part of this book and/or CD for other classrooms or for an entire school or school system is strictly prohibited. No part of this publication may be transmitted or recorded in any form without written permission from the publisher with the exception of electronic material, which may be stored on the purchaser's computer only.

Teacher Created Resources

12621 Western Avenue

Garden Grove, CA 92841

www.teachercreated.com

ISBN: 978-1-4206-3580-5

©2011 Teacher Created Resources

Reprinted, 2016

Made in U.S.A.

Table of Contents

Introduction

About this Book

The variety of math problems in *Daily Warm-Ups: Problem-Solving Math* will provide students with enough problem-solving practice to introduce your math period every day for an entire school year. For each warm-up, allow 10 to 15 minutes for reading, interpreting, and solving the problems before you correct them as a class.

Students can work on the problems in this book independently, in groups, or as a whole class. Decide which approach works best for your students, based on their math skill levels and reading competence.

The book is divided into two sections. The first section of the book introduces five specific problem-solving strategies with math problems that are not directly addressed to a specific operation or concept. The math strategies are as follows: Creating an Organized List, Making a Tree Diagram, Working Backwards, Using Simpler Numbers, and Using Logical Reasoning. (See pages 8–12 for examples of math problems to which these types of strategies apply.) The second section of the book contains more traditional problems in operations, numeration, geometry, measurement, data analysis, probability, and algebra. The general math area and focus addressed in each warm-up is noted at the top of each page.

These activities can be used in a variety of ways, but they were designed to be introductory warm-ups for each math period. The 250 warm-ups are individually numbered and should be used in any order according to your main math lessons. Choose warm-ups that cover concepts previously taught so that the warm-up can serve as a review.

Standards

The math problems in this book have been correlated to the National Council of Teachers of Mathematics (NCTM) standards and the Common Core State Standards. See the correlation chart on pages 4–7. You will find the NCTM standards and expectations along with the warm-up numbers to which they relate. As the NCTM math standards make clear, problem solving is the critical component in math instruction. It is the component that makes general operations knowledge both essential and useful. Problem solving is the basic element in the concept of math as a method of communication.

Daily Warm-Ups, Section 1

The 50 warm-ups in this section follow one of five key problem-solving strategies. Each of these pages is set up the same way, allowing students to quickly become familiar with the expectations of the problems. The answers to the problems in this section have been provided along with explanations of the thinking process behind solving each one. (See pages 163–170 for Section 1's answers.)

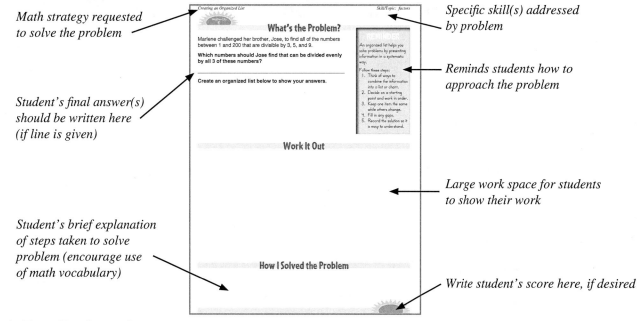

Math strategy requested to solve the problem

Student's final answer(s) should be written here (if line is given)

Student's brief explanation of steps taken to solve problem (encourage use of math vocabulary)

Specific skill(s) addressed by problem

Reminds students how to approach the problem

Large work space for students to show their work

Write student's score here, if desired

Daily Warm-Ups, Section 2

The 200 warm-ups in this section are divided into five math areas: Number and Operations, Geometry, Measurement, Data Analysis and Probability, and Algebra. Each of these pages has two warm-ups on the page. The two warm-ups relate to each other in some way. Warm-ups may be separated and given to students independently. However, in some cases, the top warm-up is needed in order to complete the bottom warm-up. Such pages are indicated with a chain symbol in the top right corner. These "linked" warm-ups should not be separated.

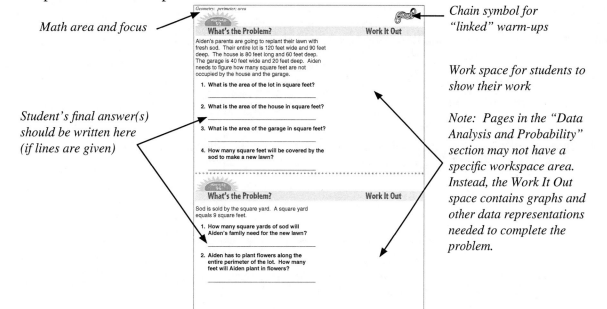

Math area and focus

Student's final answer(s) should be written here (if lines are given)

Chain symbol for "linked" warm-ups

Work space for students to show their work

Note: Pages in the "Data Analysis and Probability" section may not have a specific workspace area. Instead, the Work It Out space contains graphs and other data representations needed to complete the problem.

Correlation to Standards

The following chart lists the National Council of Teachers of Mathematics (NCTM) standards and expectations for grades 6–8. Reprinted with permission from *Principles and Standards for School Mathematics*. (Copyright 2000 by the National Council of Teachers of Mathematics. All rights reserved.) Visit *http://www.teachercreated.com/standards/* for correlations to the Common Core State Standards.

Standards and Expectations	Warm-Up Numbers
NUMBER AND OPERATIONS	
Understand numbers, ways of representing numbers, relationships among numbers, and number systems	
• Work flexibly with fractions, decimals, and percents to solve problems	30–33, 36, 38, 51–62, 65–66, 77–86, 231–232
• Compare and order fractions, decimals, and percents efficiently and find their approximate locations on a number line	51–56, 61–62, 81–88, 249–250
• Develop an understanding of large numbers and recognize and appropriately use exponential, scientific, and calculator notation	38, 43, 67–68
• Use factors, multiples, prime factorization, and relatively prime numbers to solve problems	16–17, 23, 40–41, 43, 46, 51–52, 67–68, 71–74
• Develop meaning for integers and represent and compare quantities with them	30–31, 69–70
Understand meanings of operations and how they relate to one another	
• Understand the meaning and effects of arithmetic operations with fractions, decimals, and integers	2–3, 7–9, 16–17, 19, 23, 26–29, 31–33, 35–36, 38–39, 43–47, 50–56, 65–66, 69–70, 231–232
• Use the associative and commutative properties of addition and multiplication and the distributive property of multiplication over addition to simplify computations with integers, fractions, and decimals	229–230, 247–248
• Understand and use the inverse relationships of addition and subtraction, multiplication and division, and squaring and finding square roots to simplify computations and solve problems	42, 46–48, 63–64, 75–76, 87–90, 229–230
Compute fluently and make reasonable estimates	
• Select appropriate methods and tools for computing with fractions and decimals from among mental computation, estimation, calculators or computers, and paper and pencil, depending on the situation, and apply the selected methods	32, 35, 41–42, 44, 46–48, 51, 55–56, 63–64, 71–72, 79–80
• Develop and analyze algorithms for computing with fractions, decimals, and integers and develop fluency in their use	51–62, 231–232
• Develop and use strategies to estimate the results of rational-number computations and judge the reasonableness of the results	231–232, 249–250

Standards are listed with the permission of the National Council of Teachers of Mathematics (NCTM). NCTM does not endorse the content or validity of these alignments.

Standards and Expectations	Warm-Up Numbers
GEOMETRY	
Analyze characteristics and properties of two- and three-dimensional geometric shapes and develop mathematical arguments about geometric relationships	
• Precisely describe, classify, and understand relationships among types of two- and three-dimensional objects using their defining properties	97–100, 103–104, 107–108, 123–128, 133–134
• Understand relationships among the angles, side lengths, perimeters, areas, and volumes of similar objects	45, 91–108, 121–128, 133–134, 137–140
• Create and critique inductive and deductive arguments concerning geometric ideas and relationships, such as congruence, similarity, and the Pythagorean relationship	121–122, 129–130
Specify locations and describe spatial relationships using coordinate geometry and other representational systems	
• Use coordinate geometry to represent and examine the properties of geometric shapes	113–120, 187–188, 195–196
• Use coordinate geometry to examine special geometric shapes, such as regular polygons or those with pairs of parallel or perpendicular sides	113–120, 195–196
Use visualization, spatial reasoning, and geometric modeling to solve problems	
• Draw geometric objects with specified properties, such as side lengths or angle measures	125–130
• Use two-dimensional representations of three-dimensional objects to visualize and solve problems such as those involving surface area and volume	91–92, 95–96, 103–110, 127–130, 139–140
• Use visual tools such as networks to represent and solve problems	34
• Recognize and apply geometric ideas and relationships in areas outside the mathematics classroom, such as art, science, and everyday life	75–76, 109–112, 115–120, 137–138
MEASUREMENT	
Understand measurable attributes of objects and the units, systems, and processes of measurement	
• Understand both metric and customary systems of measurement	131–134, 141–146, 157–158
• Understand relationships among units and convert from one unit to another within the same system	131–132, 143–146, 151–152, 155–158
• Understand, select, and use units of appropriate size and type to measure angles, perimeter, area, surface area, and volume	75–76, 99–102, 105–112, 141–142, 165–170

Standards and Expectations	Warm-Up Numbers
MEASUREMENT *(CONT.)*	
Apply appropriate techniques, tools, and formulas to determine measurements	
• Use common benchmarks to select appropriate methods for estimating measurements	131–132
• Select and apply techniques and tools to accurately find length, area, volume, and angle measures to appropriate levels of precision	75–76, 89–94, 99–102, 107–112, 135–136, 141–142, 147–150, 161–170
• Develop and use formulas to determine the circumference of circles and the area of triangles, parallelograms, trapezoids, and circles and develop strategies to find the area of more-complex shapes	101–112, 135–136, 139–142, 159–162, 165–170
• Develop strategies to determine the surface area and volume of selected prisms, pyramids, and cylinders	103–112, 149–150, 161–170
• Solve problems involving scale factors, using ratio and proportion	213–214
• Solve simple problems involving rates and derived measurements for such attributes as velocity and density	151–154, 157–158, 179–182, 213–214
DATA ANALYSIS AND PROBABILITY	
Formulate questions that can be addressed with data and collect, organize, and display relevant data to answer them	
• Formulate questions, design studies, and collect data about a characteristic shared by two populations or different characteristics within one population	185–192
• Select, create, and use appropriate graphical representations of data, including histograms, box plots, and scatterplots	5–6, 13–15, 171–172, 183–186, 189–190, 193–194
Select and use appropriate statistical methods to analyze data	
• Find, use, and interpret measures of center and spread, including mean and interquartile range	175–186
• Discuss and understand the correspondence between data sets and their graphical representations, especially histograms, stem-and-leaf plots, box plots, and scatterplots	171–174, 187–188, 193–194
Develop and evaluate inferences and predictions that are based on data	
• Use observations about differences between two or more samples to make conjectures about the populations from which the samples were taken	171–174, 185–186, 189–196
• Use conjectures to formulate new questions and plan new studies to answer them	171–174

Standards and Expectations	Warm-Up Numbers
DATA ANALYSIS AND PROBABILITY *(CONT.)*	
Understand and apply basic concepts of probability	
• Understand and use appropriate terminology to describe complementary and mutually exclusive events	197–210
• Use proportionality and a basic understanding of probability to make and test conjectures about the results of experiments and simulations	199–210
• Compute probabilities for simple compound events, using such methods as organized lists, tree diagrams, and area models	1–20, 22–30, 32, 34, 36–38, 40, 42, 44, 47, 49–50, 197–202
ALGEBRA	
Understand patterns, relations, and functions	
• Represent, analyze, and generalize a variety of patterns with tables, graphs, words, and, when possible, symbolic rules	7, 10–15, 18–34, 36–37, 40–44, 47, 49–50, 215–220, 225–226, 231–234, 237–238, 243–244
• Relate and compare different forms of representation for a relationship	25, 49, 211–212, 217–220, 223–224, 227–228, 231–234, 239–240, 243–244
• Identify functions as linear or nonlinear and contrast their properties from tables, graphs, or equations	231–232, 245–246
Represent and analyze mathematical situations and structures using algebraic symbols	
• Develop an initial conceptual understanding of different uses of variables	211–212, 215–220, 223–228, 233–234, 237–242
• Explore relationships between symbolic expressions and graphs of lines, paying particular attention to the meaning of intercept and slope	245–246
• Use symbolic algebra to represent situations and to solve problems, especially those that involve linear relationships	211–212, 215–218, 223–226, 237–242
• Recognize and generate equivalent forms for simple algebraic expressions and solve linear equations	211–212, 221–228
Use mathematical models to represent and understand quantitative relationships	
• Model and solve contextualized problems using various representations, such as graphs, tables, and equations	225–226, 233–244
Analyze change in various contexts	
• Use graphs to analyze the nature of changes in quantities in linear relationships	113–116

Examples of Strategies

Creating an Organized List

An organized list helps you solve problems by presenting information in a systematic way.

Follow these steps:

1. Think of ways to combine the information into a list or chart.
2. Decide on a starting point and work in order.
3. Keep one item the same while others change.
4. Fill in any gaps.
5. Record the solution so it is easy to understand.

Example 1

What's the Problem?

Liz likes to stack her stickers in an orderly way on her desk. She puts 1 sticker in the first stack, 3 stickers in the second stack, and 5 stickers in the third.

Following the same pattern, how many stickers will she place in the sixth stack?

After she makes the sixth stack, how many stickers will Liz have on her desk.

Work It Out

Stack	Stickers	Total
1	1	1
2	3	4
3	5	9
4	7	16
5	9	25
6	(11)	(36)

How I Solved the Problem

To solve the problem, a student would use the information given to fill in the first 3 rows of an organized list. In the list, the column of stickers increases by 2 each time because that is the pattern that has been established. The numbers in the "Total" column show the running total.

Example 2

What's the Problem?

Cal plays shortstop on his baseball team, while Ed plays third base, Jack plays second base, and Mike plays first base. These 4 infielders always bat in the 1–4 spots in the batting order.

List all of the possible batting orders for these 4 players when Cal bats first.

How many combinations can there be when Cal bats first and Ed bats third?

Work It Out

1st	2nd	3rd	4th
Cal	Ed	Jack	Mike
Cal	Ed	Mike	Jack
Cal	Jack	Ed	Mike
Cal	Jack	Mike	Ed
Cal	Mike	Ed	Jack
Cal	Mike	Jack	Ed

6 possible batting orders

2 combinations with Cal first and Ed third

How I Solved the Problem

To solve the problem, a student should create an organized list with one variable (Cal batting first) remaining the same throughout. A second variable (the person batting second) should also remain the same until it is used completely.

Examples of Strategies

Making a Tree Diagram

Create a tree diagram to show how the different items in a problem are connected. This strategy is helpful for solving problems where you need to find all possible combinations of the items. Begin by organizing a list of the items. Link each item into a tree diagram until all possible combinations are shown. Use the results to help solve the problem.

Example 1

What's the Problem?

In the first round of the horseshoes tournament, each member of the group had to play against each other member once. The members are Scott, Laura, Kate, Ella, and Drew.

How many games of horseshoes were played in the first round of the tournament?

Work It Out

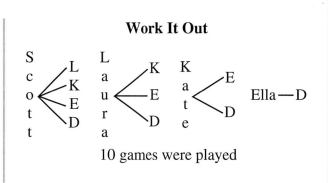

10 games were played

How I Solved the Problem

To solve the problem, a student would create tree diagrams to illustrate all of the possible combinations. The student should begin by using one player as a fixed variable and find all of the possible games that person could play. Each tree diagram thereafter should have one less "branch" representing an exchange that has already been made.

Example 2

What's the Problem?

Nick made a CD of music for 3 of his friends. Each of those friends then gave a copy of the CD to 2 more people.

How many people now have the CD (or a copy of it)?

Work It Out

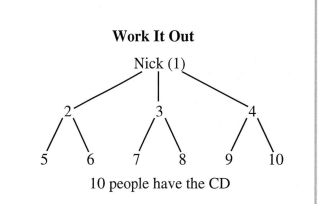

10 people have the CD

How I Solved the Problem

To solve the problem, a student would create a tree diagram to illustrate the given data. A tree diagram makes it possible to quickly show each outcome that results from each previous outcome.

Examples of Strategies

Working Backwards

Sometimes a problem seems to be written backwards. It starts with end results and asks you to solve something at the beginning. When this happens, start at the end, with the last piece of information, and work backwards (in reverse order) to find out what happened in the beginning.

Example 1

What's the Problem?

Kim, Hannah, Penny, and Eve are on the same softball team. Penny hit 7 triples, which was 3 more than Kim hit. Hannah hit 3 times as many triples as Kim but one fewer than Eve.

How many triples did each player hit?

Work It Out

Penny = 7 triples

Kim = 7 – 3 = 4 triples

Hannah = 4 x 3 = 12 triples

Eve = 12 + 1 = 13 triples

How I Solved the Problem

To solve the problem, a student would start with the end result of Penny hitting 7 triples. From there, the student can figure out Kim's total. This will lead to more answers.

Example 2

What's the Problem?

Chris was glad he brought fresh drinking water along for his 8-hour scuba diving trip. He drank 16 oz. during breakfast, 8 oz. before his dive, 12 oz. after his dive, and 24 oz. with his lunch. He then had 36 oz. left for the ride home.

How many total ounces did Chris have at the beginning of the trip?

Work It Out

16 oz. during breakfast

8 oz. before dive

12 oz. after dive

24 oz. with lunch

+ 36 oz. left
_____

96 total oz. to begin with

How I Solved the Problem

To solve the problem, a student would start with the information given and work backward to get the answer. By adding up the water used and the water left, the answer of how much water was there in the beginning can be found.

Examples of Strategies

Using Simpler Numbers

Using simpler numbers can help you solve more difficult problems. Here's how!

Replace larger numbers with smaller numbers and solve the new problem. Do this a few times until you see a pattern for solving the problem. This pattern can be shown on a table, in a picture, etc. Solve the original problem using this same pattern.

Example 1

What's the Problem?

Clay went shopping at the music store. He bought a guitar for $179, a set of strings for $13, string cleaner for $5, a strap for $21, and a set of picks for $2.

How much money did Clay spend at the music store?

Work It Out

$179 + $21 = $200

$13 + $5 + $2 = $20

$200 + $20 = $220

How I Solved the Problem

To solve the problem, a student would combine numbers together to make simpler numbers ending in 0. These simpler numbers can then be added to find the total.

Example 2

What's the Problem?

Mark tried to keep his little brother occupied for a while by asking him to add up all of the even numbers from 2–100 without using a calculator. Mark was surprised when his little brother came back with the right answer 2 minutes later.

What was his brother's answer?

Work It Out

2 + 100 = 102

4 + 98 = 102

6 + 96 = 102

etc.

Each pair of even numbers = 102

There are 50 even numbers from 2–100, so that makes 25 pairs.

25 x 102 = 2,550

How I Solved the Problem

To solve the problem, a student would combine numbers to form simpler numbers. Once the student discovers that each pair of numbers can be simplified (to 102), the problem becomes much easier to solve.

Examples of Strategies

Using Logical Reasoning

Good problem solvers learn to use logical reasoning. Begin with the idea that each piece of information is like a piece of a puzzle. Think of ways to fit the pieces together to solve the problem "puzzle." Read each "clue" carefully. Decide where to begin. Then use one or more strategies to reach a reasonable solution.

Example 1

What's the Problem?

The 4 starting linebackers on Troy's football team averaged 113 tackles. Troy led the team with 144 tackles. His friend Dave only recorded half as many tackles as Troy. Mike and Ike recorded the same number of tackles.

How many tackles did Dave, Mike, and Ike record?

Work It Out

Multiply the average (113) times number of players (4) to get the total number of tackles.

$113 \times 4 = 452$

Troy = 144 tackles

Dave = $144 \div 2 = 72$ tackles

$452 - (144 + 72) = 236$

$236 \div 2 = 118$

Mike and Ike each had 118 tackles.

How I Solved the Problem

To solve the problem, a student would use the information given to find out how many total tackles the four players had. Troy's tackles are given, and that information can be used to find Dave's tackles. Using the average number will help find the other players' stats.

Example 2

What's the Problem?

The Larson twins are almost in the middle of the class's alphabetical list of names. There are 44 students listed in alphabetical order by last name on the class's roster of names. Each student gets a number according to where he or she is listed. For example, Joe Aaron is 1 and Zoe Zucker is 44. The product of the Larson twins numbers is 342.

What numbers are the Larson twins?

Work It Out

The letter L is about halfway through the order.

$21 \times 22 = 461$ (too high)

$19 \times 20 = 380$ (too high)

$18 \times 19 = 342$ (correct answer)

The twins are numbers 18 and 19.

How I Solved the Problem

To solve the problem, a student would use the information given and their knowledge of the alphabet. Since the letter L is near the midpoint of the alphabet, one would first find the product of numbers that are about half of 44. Since the twins have the same last name, their numbers have to be consecutive.

What's the Problem?

Marlene challenged her best friend, Lauren, to make a list of all the 4-digit numbers she could think of that have the digits 9, 7, 5, and 1.

How many numbers should Lauren find?

_____

Create an organized list below to show the numbers.

REMINDER

An organized list helps you solve problems by presenting information in a systematic way.

Follow these steps:
1. Think of ways to combine the information into a list or chart.
2. Decide on a starting point and work in order.
3. Keep one item the same while others change.
4. Fill in any gaps.
5. Record the solution so it is easy to understand.

Work It Out

How I Solved the Problem

What's the Problem?

Alonzo challenged his friend, Wesley, to find 3-digit numbers that equal 90 when the digits are multiplied together. He gave one example: 295.

In the space below, list the other numbers (more than 100 and less than 1,000) that Wesley could find.

REMINDER

An organized list helps you solve problems by presenting information in a systematic way.

Follow these steps:
1. Think of ways to combine the information into a list or chart.
2. Decide on a starting point and work in order.
3. Keep one item the same while others change.
4. Fill in any gaps.
5. Record the solution so it is easy to understand.

Work It Out

How I Solved the Problem

What's the Problem?

REMINDER

An organized list helps you solve problems by presenting information in a systematic way.

Follow these steps:
1. Think of ways to combine the information into a list or chart.
2. Decide on a starting point and work in order.
3. Keep one item the same while others change.
4. Fill in any gaps.
5. Record the solution so it is easy to understand.

Many of the students at the Lincoln School carnival came to Jacqueline's booth to get change for a dollar. She didn't have any pennies or half dollars. She wondered how many different combinations of dimes, nickels, and quarters she could use to make 1 dollar in change.

How many combinations can Jacqueline find using at least 1 quarter, 1 dime, and 1 nickel?

_____

Create an organized list below to show the combinations.

Work It Out

How I Solved the Problem

What's the Problem?

Andrew wanted to find all of the palindromes between 0 and 300. He knew that a palindrome was a number that read the same from either the front or end of the number. For example, 66 is a palindrome. Likewise, 101 is a palindrome.

List all of the palindromes between 0 and 300 in the chart below.

What is the total number of palindromes?

_____

REMINDER

An organized list helps you solve problems by presenting information in a systematic way.

Follow these steps:
1. Think of ways to combine the information into a list or chart.
2. Decide on a starting point and work in order.
3. Keep one item the same while others change.
4. Fill in any gaps.
5. Record the solution so it is easy to understand.

Work It Out

Between 0 and 100	Between 101 and 200	Between 201 and 300

How I Solved the Problem

What's the Problem?

Jimmy and Allison attend a sports camp during the summer at the local college. It is open Monday through Friday. The camp runs for 4 hours a day and each activity takes 1 hour. They swim for 1 hour every day. Jimmy plays basketball 3 days a week and volleyball 2 days a week. He never plays the same sport 2 days in a row or on the same day. They must spend 1 hour reading in the children's library each day. Allison takes gymnastics every day that Jimmy plays basketball and she plays table tennis the other days. Jimmy takes tennis on the days Allison does gymnastics and he runs laps on the other days. Allison runs laps on the days she does gymnastics and she plays softball on the other days.

Create a weekly schedule of activities for each person.

An organized list helps you solve problems by presenting information in a systematic way.

Follow these steps:
1. Think of ways to combine the information into a list or chart.
2. Decide on a starting point and work in order.
3. Keep one item the same while others change.
4. Fill in any gaps.
5. Record the solution so it is easy to understand.

Work It Out

Jimmy

Monday	Tuesday	Wednesday	Thursday	Friday

Allison

Monday	Tuesday	Wednesday	Thursday	Friday

How I Solved the Problem

Warm-Up
6

What's the Problem?

The art teacher at Glenhaven School asked each student to create a drawing of an imaginary animal from 2 real animals. She gave the students 5 different animals to choose from: dog, cat, mouse, alligator, and bird. They can use each of the real animals to make either the front or back of the imaginary animal.

How many possible combinations can the students make?

_____

Make an organized list below showing the different possible combinations.

REMINDER

An organized list helps you solve problems by presenting information in a systematic way.

Follow these steps:
1. Think of ways to combine the information into a list or chart.
2. Decide on a starting point and work in order.
3. Keep one item the same while others change.
4. Fill in any gaps.
5. Record the solution so it is easy to understand.

Work It Out

How I Solved the Problem

Warm-Up 7

What's the Problem?

REMINDER

An organized list helps you solve problems by presenting information in a systematic way.

Follow these steps:
1. Think of ways to combine the information into a list or chart.
2. Decide on a starting point and work in order.
3. Keep one item the same while others change.
4. Fill in any gaps.
5. Record the solution so it is easy to understand.

Mark's dad had a big bucket full of pennies. He offered Mark a deal if Mark would help organize the pennies. Mark's dad challenged him to place the pennies in bags in an organized way. Mark had to place 1 penny in the first bag. He would place 2 pennies in the next bag, 4 pennies in the bag after that, and 8 pennies in the following bag. Mark was to follow the same pattern placing pennies in just 21 bags. If Mark did it right, his father would let him use the pennies from the 21st bag toward his college savings account.

How many pennies did Mark place in the 21st bag?

_____

How much money did he receive?

_____

Create an organized list below to show your answers.

Work It Out

How I Solved the Problem

Warm-Up 8

What's the Problem?

Marlene challenged her brother, Jose, to find all of the numbers between 1 and 200 that are divisible by 3, 5, and 9.

Which numbers should Jose find that can be divided evenly by all 3 of these numbers?

_____

Create an organized list below to show your answers.

REMINDER

An organized list helps you solve problems by presenting information in a systematic way.

Follow these steps:
1. Think of ways to combine the information into a list or chart.
2. Decide on a starting point and work in order.
3. Keep one item the same while others change.
4. Fill in any gaps.
5. Record the solution so it is easy to understand.

Work It Out

How I Solved the Problem

What's the Problem?

Kathy was asked to pile the quarters taken in from extra drink sales during a heat wave at school. She placed 1 quarter in the first pile, 4 quarters in the second pile, and 7 quarters in the third pile.

Following the same pattern, how many quarters did she place in the 8th pile?

_____

How many quarters did she use in all 8 piles altogether?

_____

Create an organized list below to show your answers.

REMINDER

An organized list helps you solve problems by presenting information in a systematic way.

Follow these steps:
1. Think of ways to combine the information into a list or chart.
2. Decide on a starting point and work in order.
3. Keep one item the same while others change.
4. Fill in any gaps.
5. Record the solution so it is easy to understand.

Work It Out

How I Solved the Problem

Warm-Up 10

What's the Problem?

David was playing a card game with only the 13 cards in hearts out of the full deck. The Jack, Queen, and King of hearts were each valued at 10 points. The Ace was valued at 11 points. Each number card in hearts from 2 to 10 was the value shown on the card. The best hand to have was 2 cards whose value together equaled 13.

How many combinations of 2 heart cards could equal 13?

_____

Make an organized list below to show the possible combinations.

REMINDER

An organized list helps you solve problems by presenting information in a systematic way.

Follow these steps:
1. Think of ways to combine the information into a list or chart.
2. Decide on a starting point and work in order.
3. Keep one item the same while others change.
4. Fill in any gaps.
5. Record the solution so it is easy to understand.

Work It Out

How I Solved the Problem

Warm-Up 11

What's the Problem?

The 8 members of the Super Secret Science Club have a special handshake. Each member of the club—Justin, Gary, Patrick, Daniel, Noah, Bill, Michael, and Chris—must shake hands using their special handshake with every other member before meetings begin.

How many total handshakes will they make before each meeting?

_____

Make tree diagrams in the space below to show the possibilities.

REMINDER

Create a tree diagram to show how the different items in a problem are connected. This strategy is helpful for solving problems where you need to find all possible combinations of the items. Begin by organizing a list of the items. Link each item into a tree diagram until all possible combinations are shown. Use the results to help solve the problem.

Work It Out

How I Solved the Problem

What's the Problem?

REMINDER
Create a tree diagram to show how the different items in a problem are connected. This strategy is helpful for solving problems where you need to find all possible combinations of the items. Begin by organizing a list of the items. Link each item into a tree diagram until all possible combinations are shown. Use the results to help solve the problem.

Ava comes from a large family. During the holiday season, the 10 members of the family—Mom, Dad, Ava, Sara, Catherine, James, Harry, Kevin, Eric, and Linda—each give every other member of the family a present.

Make tree diagrams in the space below to illustrate the gift exchange for all 10 members of the family.

How many total gift exchanges will Ava's family make?

_____

Work It Out

How I Solved the Problem

What's the Problem?

The 32 members of the exercise club at Theodore Roosevelt School had an arm-wrestling tournament that was supervised by the coach. The winners of each round competed against each other until a final winner was remaining.

Create a tree diagram in the space below to illustrate how many rounds it took to find the winner.

How many rounds did it take to find a winner?

_____

REMINDER

Create a tree diagram to show how the different items in a problem are connected. This strategy is helpful for solving problems where you need to find all possible combinations of the items. Begin by organizing a list of the items. Link each item into a tree diagram until all possible combinations are shown. Use the results to help solve the problem.

Work It Out

How I Solved the Problem

What's the Problem?

REMINDER

Create a tree diagram to show how the different items in a problem are connected. This strategy is helpful for solving problems where you need to find all possible combinations of the items. Begin by organizing a list of the items. Link each item into a tree diagram until all possible combinations are shown. Use the results to help solve the problem.

Samantha went on a wonderful shopping trip with her mother to buy new clothes. She doesn't like to wear exactly the same outfit every day. She bought 4 blouses: flaming red, deep blue, lavender, and striped. She bought blue jeans, a polka-dotted skirt, pink capris, black shorts, and a skort. She also got a sports cap with her favorite team logo and a cap with her future college logo. Samantha always wears a cap.

Make tree diagrams in the space below showing how many days Samantha can wear a different outfit without repeating exactly the same combination of clothes in her outfit.

What is the total number of outfits?

_____

Work It Out

How I Solved the Problem

What's the Problem?

On Tuesday morning, Marlene told her best friend, Nadine, about a secret surprise party that was being held for their student teacher. No student was supposed to know about the party until it actually began at 2:00 that afternoon. However, Nadine told 2 friends and each of them told 2 friends. Each of these friends told 2 more friends, who then told 1 friend each. So by the afternoon, 24 people knew about the party.

Make a tree diagram in the space below to illustrate how the secret spread from Marlene to 23 other people.

REMINDER

Create a tree diagram to show how the different items in a problem are connected. This strategy is helpful for solving problems where you need to find all possible combinations of the items. Begin by organizing a list of the items. Link each item into a tree diagram until all possible combinations are shown. Use the results to help solve the problem.

Work It Out

How I Solved the Problem

Warm-Up 16

What's the Problem?

Eileen and Anne had a discussion about which number—72 or 96—had the greatest number of prime factors. Eileen thought that 72 had more prime factors. Anne said it had to be 96 because it was larger.

Make tree diagrams (factor trees) in the space below showing all of the prime factors of each number. (The numbers on the final branches of the tree are all counted as prime factors even if they are repeated.)

Which number had the most prime factors?

_____

REMINDER

Create a tree diagram to show how the different items in a problem are connected. This strategy is helpful for solving problems where you need to find all possible combinations of the items. Begin by organizing a list of the items. Link each item into a tree diagram until all possible combinations are shown. Use the results to help solve the problem.

Work It Out

How I Solved the Problem

Warm-Up 17

What's the Problem?

Alfred and Raphael had a discussion about the largest number of prime factors in a number less than 1,000. Alfred said 999 would have a lot of prime factors. Raphael said 144 would have more than 999.

Use tree diagrams to determine which number has more prime factors. (The numbers on all of the end branches of the tree are prime and count even if they are repeated.) Draw them in the space below.

How many prime factors did each of their numbers have?

_____

Which number had more?

_____

> **REMINDER**
>
> Create a tree diagram to show how the different items in a problem are connected. This strategy is helpful for solving problems where you need to find all possible combinations of the items. Begin by organizing a list of the items. Link each item into a tree diagram until all possible combinations are shown. Use the results to help solve the problem.

Work It Out

How I Solved the Problem

Warm-Up
18

What's the Problem?

When the twins, Sandy and Mandy, were walking to school, their best friend, Lorraine, told them a secret. Sandy and Mandy each then told the secret to 2 more friends. In turn, each of those friends told the secret to 2 more friends.

If the twins are the first set of friends who found out about the secret and if this pattern continues, how many people will know the secret after the 4th set of friends are told?

_____

Make a tree diagram in the space below to show how the secret spread.

REMINDER

Create a tree diagram to show how the different items in a problem are connected. This strategy is helpful for solving problems where you need to find all possible combinations of the items. Begin by organizing a list of the items. Link each item into a tree diagram until all possible combinations are shown. Use the results to help solve the problem.

Work It Out

How I Solved the Problem

What's the Problem?

Kevin created a model tree diagram using pennies. The top of the diagram had 1 penny that had 3 branches. Each branch then had 3 more branches, and then each of these branches had 3 more branches. There was 1 penny on each branch.

How many pennies did Kevin use if he had 4 levels of pennies in his diagram?

_____

Draw Kevin's tree diagram in the space below.

REMINDER

Create a tree diagram to show how the different items in a problem are connected. This strategy is helpful for solving problems where you need to find all possible combinations of the items. Begin by organizing a list of the items. Link each item into a tree diagram until all possible combinations are shown. Use the results to help solve the problem.

Work It Out

How I Solved the Problem

What's the Problem?

Wesley rides his bike to school every day. One Monday afternoon, Wesley couldn't remember the code to his bike's combination lock. He knew that the numbers in the code were 7, 9, 5, and 2, but he couldn't remember the correct order.

Make tree diagrams in the space below to show the possible combinations for the bike lock code.

How many possible combinations could the lock have?

_____

REMINDER

Create a tree diagram to show how the different items in a problem are connected. This strategy is helpful for solving problems where you need to find all possible combinations of the items. Begin by organizing a list of the items. Link each item into a tree diagram until all possible combinations are shown. Use the results to help solve the problem.

Work It Out

How I Solved the Problem

What's the Problem?

The girls in Miss Stanton's class were comparing the number of books they read. Alicia read 14 more books than Irene. Mary read 6 less books than Irene, but 9 more books than Kathy. Alicia and Sarah together read 71 books. Jolene read 7 fewer books than Sarah, who read 41 books. Maybeth read twice as many books as Mary.

How many books did each girl read?

_____

_____

_____

_____

Use the space below to solve the problem.

REMINDER

Sometimes a problem seems to be written backwards. It starts with end results and asks you to solve something at the beginning. When this happens, start at the end, with the last piece of information, and work backwards (in reverse order) to find out what happened in the beginning.

Work It Out

How I Solved the Problem

What's the Problem?

Carlos was playing a board game in which the object was to have the most play money at the end of the game. He paid $5,000 to buy a piece of property on the board. He received $1,000 in rent and paid $4,000 in taxes. Then he lost half of his remaining money in a bad land deal. After this, he only had $3,000 left.

How much money did he have at the beginning of the game?

_____

Use the space below to solve the problem.

> **REMINDER**
>
> Sometimes a problem seems to be written backwards. It starts with end results and asks you to solve something at the beginning. When this happens, start at the end, with the last piece of information, and work backwards (in reverse order) to find out what happened in the beginning.

Work It Out

How I Solved the Problem

What's the Problem?

REMINDER

Sometimes a problem seems to be written backwards. It starts with end results and asks you to solve something at the beginning. When this happens, start at the end, with the last piece of information, and work backwards (in reverse order) to find out what happened in the beginning.

Kevin posed this problem to his buddy, Julian: "I am thinking of a number. It is greater than 500 and less than 800. It is evenly divisible by 2, 4, 5, 9, and 10. It does not have a 2 in the number. What is the number?"

What is Kevin's number?

_____

Use the space below to solve the problem.

Work It Out

How I Solved the Problem

What's the Problem?

There are 7 brothers in Jeffrey's family. Jeremiah is 2 years older than Jeffrey, but 3 years younger than Justin. James is 2 years younger than Jeffrey and 3 years older than Jack. Jack is 2 years older than Jonathan, who is 1 year old. Jordan and Jeremiah are twins.

What are the ages of each boy?

_____

_____

_____

_____

Use the space below to solve the problem.

REMINDER

Sometimes a problem seems to be written backwards. It starts with end results and asks you to solve something at the beginning. When this happens, start at the end, with the last piece of information, and work backwards (in reverse order) to find out what happened in the beginning.

Work It Out

How I Solved the Problem

What's the Problem?

George put 143 pennies in 10 piles. The last pile had 55 pennies.
The 9th pile had 34 pennies, and the 8th pile had 21 pennies.
The 6th pile had 8 pennies.

How many pennies were in each of the 10 piles?

_____

_____

_____

What is the pattern?

_____

**Use the space below to solve the problem and show
your answers.**

REMINDER

Sometimes a problem seems to be written backwards. It starts with end results and asks you to solve something at the beginning. When this happens, start at the end, with the last piece of information, and work backwards (in reverse order) to find out what happened in the beginning.

Work It Out

How I Solved the Problem

What's the Problem?

Cindy came to school with a bag of birthday candy bars to share with her friends. She gave half of her candy to her best friend, Ashley. She then gave half of the remaining candy bars to her other best friend, Samantha. Next, Cindy gave half of the remaining candy bars to her friend Jackie. Cindy kept the remaining 8 candy bars for herself.

How many candy bars did each friend receive?

_____

_____

How many candy bars did Cindy start with in the bag?

_____

Use the space below to solve the problem.

REMINDER

Sometimes a problem seems to be written backwards. It starts with end results and asks you to solve something at the beginning. When this happens, start at the end, with the last piece of information, and work backwards (in reverse order) to find out what happened in the beginning.

Work It Out

How I Solved the Problem

Warm-Up
27

What's the Problem?

Marcie has a chain with 33 charms on it. Every year, she receives 3 charms in March on her birthday, 2 charms for Christmas, and 1 at Easter. Marcie just celebrated her 11th birthday.

How old was Marcie when she received her first charms on her birthday?

_____

How many charms will she receive on the next celebration?

_____

What occasion will the gift celebrate?

_____

Use the space below to solve the problem.

REMINDER

Sometimes a problem seems to be written backwards. It starts with end results and asks you to solve something at the beginning. When this happens, start at the end, with the last piece of information, and work backwards (in reverse order) to find out what happened in the beginning.

Work It Out

How I Solved the Problem

What's the Problem?

Josiah was playing a card game in which the first player received half of 128 points. The next player received half of the remaining points. Each player in order received half of the remaining points.

How many players could earn points? (Point values must be whole numbers.)

_____

How many points did the last player receive?

_____

Use the space below to solve the problem.

REMINDER

Sometimes a problem seems to be written backwards. It starts with end results and asks you to solve something at the beginning. When this happens, start at the end, with the last piece of information, and work backwards (in reverse order) to find out what happened in the beginning.

Work It Out

How I Solved the Problem

What's the Problem?

James had all of his money saved in a metal can in his room. He spent half of his total savings to buy a dirt bike. He spent half of the money he had left to buy a helmet and racing outfit. He spent $25 on a gift for his parents. In the end, James only had $75 left.

How much money did James have in his savings can to start with?

_____

Use the space below to solve the problem.

> **REMINDER**
>
> Sometimes a problem seems to be written backwards. It starts with end results and asks you to solve something at the beginning. When this happens, start at the end, with the last piece of information, and work backwards (in reverse order) to find out what happened in the beginning.

Work It Out

How I Solved the Problem

What's the Problem?

Kristin was playing a card game with her best friends using a total of 126 cards. At the end of the game, Kristin had twice as many cards as Jennifer. Yvonne had half as many cards as Jennifer. Briana had half as many cards as Yvonne, and twice as many cards as Sarah. Sarah had twice as many cards as Hannah, who had 2 cards.

How many cards did each girl have?

_____

_____

_____

Use the space below to solve the problem.

REMINDER

Sometimes a problem seems to be written backwards. It starts with end results and asks you to solve something at the beginning. When this happens, start at the end, with the last piece of information, and work backwards (in reverse order) to find out what happened in the beginning.

Work It Out

How I Solved the Problem

What's the Problem?

REMINDER

Jonathan's teacher gave him a classroom assignment to add all of the numbers from 1 to 100 without a calculator. Jonathan finished the assignment in 30 seconds. His correct answer was 5,050.

Use a method of simplifying the numbers to find how Jonathan got the correct answer.

Show and describe your method in the space below.

Using simpler numbers can help you solve more difficult problems. Here's how!

Replace larger numbers with smaller numbers and solve the new problem. Do this a few times until you see a pattern for solving the problem. This pattern can be shown on a table, in a picture, etc. Solve the original problem using this same pattern.

Work It Out

How I Solved the Problem

Warm-Up 32

What's the Problem?

April went shopping with her mom before their family vacation. April bought a skirt for $17.99, a dress for $22.99, a pair of shoes for $59.99, a shirt for $9.99, and a winter coat for $119.99.

Use simpler numbers to determine the total cost of April's purchases. What was the total cost of her purchases before tax?

_____

Use the space below to solve the problem and show your answers.

REMINDER

Using simpler numbers can help you solve more difficult problems. Here's how!

Replace larger numbers with smaller numbers and solve the new problem. Do this a few times until you see a pattern for solving the problem. This pattern can be shown on a table, in a picture, etc. Solve the original problem using this same pattern.

Work It Out

How I Solved the Problem

What's the Problem?

Archer needed an estimated total for these receipts: $0.23, $0.54, $0.77, $0.50, $0.21, $0.47, $0.73, $0.99, $0.49, $1.06, $0.27, $0.48, and $1.02.

Use simpler numbers to find an estimated total for the receipts.

Find a system using simpler numbers to find the exact total. (Hint: Look for pairs of numbers that, when added, make a simpler number, e.g., .23 + .77 = 1.00)

Use the space below to solve the problem and show your answers.

REMINDER

Using simpler numbers can help you solve more difficult problems. Here's how!

Replace larger numbers with smaller numbers and solve the new problem. Do this a few times until you see a pattern for solving the problem. This pattern can be shown on a table, in a picture, etc. Solve the original problem using this same pattern.

Work It Out

How I Solved the Problem

Warm-Up 34

What's the Problem?

Nicole is building a fence out of toothpicks for her school project. The fence is made up of a series of square sections. Each square section is made with 4 toothpicks.

How many toothpicks will Nicole need to make a fence that is 7 sections long?

_____

Use the space below to solve the problem.

REMINDER

Using simpler numbers can help you solve more difficult problems. Here's how!

Replace larger numbers with smaller numbers and solve the new problem. Do this a few times until you see a pattern for solving the problem. This pattern can be shown on a table, in a picture, etc. Solve the original problem using this same pattern.

Work It Out

How I Solved the Problem

Warm-Up 35

What's the Problem?

Jasmine wanted to quickly add all of the money collected by her class in the school jog-a-thon. These were the amounts:

$11	$13	$79
$19	$8	$21
$27	$22	

What simple method can you use to quickly add all of the numbers?

_____

_____

What is the total?

_____

Use the space below to solve the problem.

REMINDER

Using simpler numbers can help you solve more difficult problems. Here's how!

Replace larger numbers with smaller numbers and solve the new problem. Do this a few times until you see a pattern for solving the problem. This pattern can be shown on a table, in a picture, etc. Solve the original problem using this same pattern.

Work It Out

How I Solved the Problem

What's the Problem?

Jeffrey collected money for ice cream sandwiches in the cafeteria during a heat wave. These were the amounts he collected: $1.50, $0.75, $0.55, $0.22, $0.28, $0.20, $0.75, $0.50, and $1.75.

Simplify the numbers to rapidly total the amounts.

What is the estimated total?

_____

Use the space below to solve the problem.

REMINDER

Using simpler numbers can help you solve more difficult problems. Here's how!

Replace larger numbers with smaller numbers and solve the new problem. Do this a few times until you see a pattern for solving the problem. This pattern can be shown on a table, in a picture, etc. Solve the original problem using this same pattern.

Work It Out

How I Solved the Problem

What's the Problem?

REMINDER

At a family reunion, Jill and her 11 cousins were expected to greet each other before they went outside to play. The other cousins are named: Mary, Larry, Sarah, Maria, Joey, Kenny, Cindy, Sammy, Jane, Regis, and Tony.

If they greeted each other in order, how many greetings did each cousin give?

_____

How many greetings were given all together?

_____

Use the space below to solve the problem and show your answers.

Using simpler numbers can help you solve more difficult problems. Here's how!

Replace larger numbers with smaller numbers and solve the new problem. Do this a few times until you see a pattern for solving the problem. This pattern can be shown on a table, in a picture, etc. Solve the original problem using this same pattern.

Work It Out

How I Solved the Problem

Warm-Up 38

What's the Problem?

Jonah's homework was to total all of the even numbers from 900 to 1,000.

How many numbers will he add?

_____

What simple method could he use to add the numbers?

_____

What is the total?

_____

Use the space below to solve the problem.

REMINDER

Using simpler numbers can help you solve more difficult problems. Here's how!

Replace larger numbers with smaller numbers and solve the new problem. Do this a few times until you see a pattern for solving the problem. This pattern can be shown on a table, in a picture, etc. Solve the original problem using this same pattern.

Work It Out

How I Solved the Problem

What's the Problem?

It took David exactly 99 digits (0 to 9) to number the pages in his famous person report.

How many pages were in his report? (Hint: Simplify the numbers and make an organized list.)

_____

Use the space below to solve the problem.

REMINDER

Using simpler numbers can help you solve more difficult problems. Here's how!

Replace larger numbers with smaller numbers and solve the new problem. Do this a few times until you see a pattern for solving the problem. This pattern can be shown on a table, in a picture, etc. Solve the original problem using this same pattern.

Work It Out

How I Solved the Problem

Warm-Up
40

What's the Problem?

Phillip discovered an organism that doubled in weight every 3 minutes. It started out weighing only half a gram.

How many grams did it weigh after 30 minutes?

_____

Use simple numbers and organize a chart in the space below to help you solve this problem.

REMINDER

Using simpler numbers can help you solve more difficult problems. Here's how!

Replace larger numbers with smaller numbers and solve the new problem. Do this a few times until you see a pattern for solving the problem. This pattern can be shown on a table, in a picture, etc. Solve the original problem using this same pattern.

Work It Out

How I Solved the Problem

What's the Problem?

Four boys played on the Painterville Packers Pony League team. The numbers on their jerseys were 64, 17, 6, and 4. Edgar's number is the cubic root of Elijah's number. Eugene's number is the product of the first 3 counting numbers. Ernest's number has only 2 factors.

Which number did each boy wear?

_____

_____

Use the space below to solve the problem.

REMINDER

Good problem solvers learn to use logical reasoning. Begin with the idea that each piece of information is like a piece of a puzzle. Think of ways to fit the pieces together to solve the problem "puzzle." Read each "clue" carefully. Decide where to begin. Then use one or more strategies to reach a reasonable solution.

Work It Out

How I Solved the Problem

Warm-Up
42

What's the Problem?

Five girls, Cheryl, Mariah, Jewel, Alexis, and Madison, played for the local girls basketball team. Their jersey numbers were 1, 36, 13, 66, and 45. The girls' numbers correspond to their heights, with the shortest girl wearing the number with the least value and the tallest girl wearing the number with the greatest value. Mariah is taller than Jewel, but not as tall as Madison. Cheryl is shorter than Jewel. Alexis wears a number whose square and square root are the same number.

Which number does each girl wear?

_____

_____

Use the space below to solve the problem.

> **REMINDER**
>
> Good problem solvers learn to use logical reasoning. Begin with the idea that each piece of information is like a piece of a puzzle. Think of ways to fit the pieces together to solve the problem "puzzle." Read each "clue" carefully. Decide where to begin. Then use one or more strategies to reach a reasonable solution.

Work It Out

How I Solved the Problem

What's the Problem?

Hazel, Sandy, Dixie, and April averaged their latest math scores. The average was 87%.   April scored 100%. Dixie scored 82%. Sandy and Hazel had the same score.

What were Sandy and Hazel's scores?

_____

Use the space below to solve the problem.

> **REMINDER**
>
> Good problem solvers learn to use logical reasoning. Begin with the idea that each piece of information is like a piece of a puzzle. Think of ways to fit the pieces together to solve the problem "puzzle." Read each "clue" carefully. Decide where to begin. Then use one or more strategies to reach a reasonable solution.

Work It Out

How I Solved the Problem

Warm-Up 44

What's the Problem?

Ricky read the odometer on his father's car. It read 23,932 miles. He noticed that the number was a palindrome. It read the same backwards as forwards.

What is the next number on the odometer that would be a palindrome?

_____

Use the space below to solve the problem.

REMINDER

Good problem solvers learn to use logical reasoning. Begin with the idea that each piece of information is like a piece of a puzzle. Think of ways to fit the pieces together to solve the problem "puzzle." Read each "clue" carefully. Decide where to begin. Then use one or more strategies to reach a reasonable solution.

Work It Out

How I Solved the Problem

What's the Problem?

Jamie's little brother has a set of building toys with 160 blocks that are 2 centimeters wide, 1 centimeter high, and 4 centimeters long.

What are the measurements of a box that will hold all 160 blocks? (The box cannot be smaller than 6 centimeters on any side.)

_____

Use the space below to solve the problem.

> ### REMINDER
>
> Good problem solvers learn to use logical reasoning. Begin with the idea that each piece of information is like a piece of a puzzle. Think of ways to fit the pieces together to solve the problem "puzzle." Read each "clue" carefully. Decide where to begin. Then use one or more strategies to reach a reasonable solution.

Work It Out

How I Solved the Problem

Warm-Up 46

What's the Problem?

REMINDER

Good problem solvers learn to use logical reasoning. Begin with the idea that each piece of information is like a piece of a puzzle. Think of ways to fit the pieces together to solve the problem "puzzle." Read each "clue" carefully. Decide where to begin. Then use one or more strategies to reach a reasonable solution.

Peter proposed this puzzle to his friends: "What is the largest single-digit number that will divide evenly into each of the following numbers without a remainder?"

321,456,330   999,333,108

111,123,630   459,954,342

What is the answer to Peter's puzzle?

_____

Use the space below to solve the problem.

Work It Out

How I Solved the Problem

Warm-Up
47

What's the Problem?

Jerry passed a note to Allison that read, "My favorite reading book of the moment has 389 pages. The product of the numbers on the two facing pages I'm reading right now is 8,372. Can you figure out what pages my book is open to?" Allison looked at Jerry from across the room and noticed that Jerry was about a quarter of the way through the book.

Help her find the pages Jerry is on at the moment. (You may use a calculator.)

_____

Use the space below to solve the problem.

> **REMINDER**
>
> Good problem solvers learn to use logical reasoning. Begin with the idea that each piece of information is like a piece of a puzzle. Think of ways to fit the pieces together to solve the problem "puzzle." Read each "clue" carefully. Decide where to begin. Then use one or more strategies to reach a reasonable solution.

Work It Out

How I Solved the Problem

What's the Problem?

Jackie lives on a farm with cows and chickens. She has 41 animals that have a total of 110 legs altogether.

How many cows and how many chickens does she have on her farm?

_____

Use the space below to solve the problem.

REMINDER

Good problem solvers learn to use logical reasoning. Begin with the idea that each piece of information is like a piece of a puzzle. Think of ways to fit the pieces together to solve the problem "puzzle." Read each "clue" carefully. Decide where to begin. Then use one or more strategies to reach a reasonable solution.

Work It Out

How I Solved the Problem

Warm-Up
49

What's the Problem?

Jasmine (age 8), James (age 7), and Anna (age 5) went to the mall with their mother, Cherrie, and had lunch at Burgers Galore in the food court. They each had a drink, a side order, and one topping for the burger. None of them bought the same drink, side order, or topping. Mother had tomatoes. James had curly fries and ketchup. He does not like the taste of lemon. Jasmine had cheese fries and Anna had lettuce. The youngest child was told to drink milk. No one ordered a drink or side order that began with the same letter as his or her name.

What did each person order?

Drinks	Side Orders	Toppings
cola	regular fries	ketchup
lemonade	curly fries	barbeque sauce
juice	cheese fries	lettuce
milk	chips	tomatoes

Use the space below to solve the problem and show your answers.

REMINDER

Good problem solvers learn to use logical reasoning. Begin with the idea that each piece of information is like a piece of a puzzle. Think of ways to fit the pieces together to solve the problem "puzzle." Read each "clue" carefully. Decide where to begin. Then use one or more strategies to reach a reasonable solution.

Work It Out

How I Solved the Problem

Warm-Up
50

What's the Problem?

Alicia added up the ages of herself and her 3 sisters: Amy, Allison, and Alexis. The sum of their ages equaled their mother's age. Alicia is 2 years older than Amy and 10 years older than Alexis. Allison is 5 years old, and 2 years older than Alexis.

How old is each girl?

_____

_____

How old is their mother?

_____

Use the space below to solve the problem.

REMINDER

Good problem solvers learn to use logical reasoning. Begin with the idea that each piece of information is like a piece of a puzzle. Think of ways to fit the pieces together to solve the problem "puzzle." Read each "clue" carefully. Decide where to begin. Then use one or more strategies to reach a reasonable solution.

Work It Out

How I Solved the Problem

Warm-Up 51

What's the Problem?

Work It Out

Jade and Jasmine were trying to reduce the fraction $\frac{48}{60}$ by finding the greatest common factor. They looked for the largest number that would divide evenly into both the numerator (48) and the denominator (60).

1. **What is the largest number that will divide into both parts of the faction?**

   _____

2. **What is the reduced fraction?**

   _____

3. **Use the same system to find the greatest common factor and reduce the fraction $\frac{38}{48}$.**

   _____

- -

Warm-Up 52

What's the Problem?

Work It Out

Jasmine said she had a system for finding the greatest common factor for reducing fractions that often worked—although not always. She subtracted the numerator from the denominator and tried the difference to see if it would reduce both parts of the fraction. She used the example $\frac{24}{36}$. The difference between 24 and 36 is 12, and 12 is the greatest common factor of those 2 numbers.

Decide which of these fractions can be reduced to lowest terms using Jasmine's system. Circle those that can.

A. $\frac{48}{60}$ D. $\frac{14}{16}$ G. $\frac{90}{100}$

B. $\frac{8}{12}$ E. $\frac{21}{24}$ H. $\frac{32}{38}$

C. $\frac{9}{15}$ F. $\frac{26}{39}$

Warm-Up 53

What's the Problem?   **Work It Out**

Jeremiah ate $\frac{3}{16}$ of a pepperoni pizza.

His younger sister, Emily, ate $\frac{1}{8}$ of the pizza.

His older sister, Kari, ate $\frac{1}{4}$ of the pizza.

1. Who ate the most pizza?

_____

2. How much pizza did the 3 siblings eat altogether?

_____

3. How much pizza was left?

_____

Warm-Up 54

What's the Problem?   **Work It Out**

Emily ate $\frac{1}{3}$ of a chocolate cake. Kari ate $\frac{2}{5}$ of the cake, and Jeremiah ate $\frac{4}{15}$ of the cake.

1. Who ate the most cake?

_____

2. How much cake did the 3 siblings eat altogether?

_____

3. How much cake was left?

_____

Warm-Up 55

What's the Problem?

Work It Out

Justin has $\frac{1}{4}$ of a dollar. Jason has $\frac{3}{5}$ of a dollar. Jake has 0.65 of a dollar, and Joshua has 0.4 of a dollar.

How much money in dollars and cents do they have altogether?

_____

Warm-Up 56

What's the Problem?

Work It Out

After receiving their allowances, Justin spent 1.3 dollars on candy. Jason spent $\frac{4}{10}$ of a dollar on gum. Jake spent 0.6 of a dollar on a comic, and Joshua spent $\frac{3}{4}$ of a dollar on a used yo-yo.

How much money in dollars and cents did they spend in all?

_____

Warm-Up 57

What's the Problem?

Work It Out

Matthew took a long, end-of-the-book math test with 75 problems. He got 76% of the problems correct.

1. How many problems did he get right?

_____

2. What percent did he get wrong?

_____

Warm-Up 58

What's the Problem?

Work It Out

On a final reading test, Matthew got 80% of the 40 questions correct.

1. How many questions did he get right?

_____

2. How many questions did he miss?

_____

3. What percent did he get wrong?

_____

Warm-Up 59

What's the Problem?

Work It Out

Yvonne bought a bag with 60 chocolate-coated marshmallow cookies. She gave $\frac{1}{4}$ of the cookies to her sister, Ruth. She gave $\frac{1}{3}$ of them to her brother, Jess, and 20% to her best friend, Angie.

1. **How many cookies did she give away?**

   _____

2. **How many cookies does she have left?**

   _____

3. **What percent of the total does she still have?**

   _____

· ·

Warm-Up 60

What's the Problem?

Work It Out

Yvonne's mother bought a bag with 50 chocolate candies shaped like teardrops. She gave Ruth 12% of the candies, and Jess got 0.2 of the candies. Yvonne received 0.32 of the candies.

1. **How many candies did each child receive?**

   _____

   _____

2. **How many candies were left?**

   _____

3. **What percentage of the candies were left?**

   _____

Warm-Up 61

What's the Problem?

Work It Out

Amy went shopping for clothes at her favorite store in the mall, Girls on the Go. She bought a blouse for $32 and a pair of stylish jeans for $44. She received a discount of 20% off the total sale.

1. **How much was the discount?**

   _____

2. **What was the final cost of the outfit before sales tax?**

   _____

Warm-Up 62

What's the Problem?

Work It Out

Amy's mother bought her a pair of tennis shoes for school that were priced at $32.88 before a 25% discount.

1. **How much money did Amy's mother save because of the discount?**

   _____

2. **What was the final cost of the tennis shoes before sales tax?**

   _____

Warm-Up 63

What's the Problem?

Work It Out

Jason told his friends that he could tell if a number was divisible by 9 just by adding the digits in the number. He pointed out that in the number 18, 1 + 8 = 9 and 9 divides evenly into 18. Jason listed some numbers and challenged his friends to find one number where it didn't work.

Jason's numbers: 333

126,063

277,227

111,222,333

345,678,678

Check each of Jason's numbers to see if his system works. What is the quotient when each of the above numbers is divided by 9?

Write the quotients next to the numbers.

• •

Warm-Up 64

What's the Problem?

Work It Out

Petra told Jason she had found one other number less than 10 that has the same divisibility rule as 9. She could add the digits to tell if the number was divisible by that divisor. She challenged Jason to find that number greater than 1 but less than 10.

Find the number Petra has found. Try each number between 2 and 8.

_____

Warm-Up 65

What's the Problem?

Work It Out

Anthony mixed $\frac{7}{30}$ of a cup of water with $\frac{5}{18}$ of a cup of vinegar in a science experiment.

1. **How much more vinegar than water did Anthony use?**

   _____

2. **What was the total amount of fluid in the mixture?**

   _____

Warm-Up 66

What's the Problem?

Work It Out

Anthony created a solution with $\frac{7}{9}$ of a cup of water, $\frac{1}{18}$ of a cup of rubbing alcohol, and $\frac{1}{6}$ of a cup of soap.

What was the total amount of liquid in his solution?

_____

Warm-Up 67

What's the Problem?

Work It Out

Jacob was very interested in extreme distances and did not want to have to write long numbers in his essay describing the distances of planets from the sun. He knew that Mercury was 36,000,000 miles from the sun. He wrote the number as 3.6×10^7 (10 to the 7th power). He created a chart to show the distances from the planets to the sun in scientific notation.

Complete Jacob's chart.

Planet	Distance from the Sun (miles)	Distance in Scientific Notation
Mercury	36,000,000	A. 3.6×10^7
Venus	67,000,000	B.
Earth	93,000,000	C.
Mars	141,000,000	D. 1.41×10^8
Jupiter	480,000,000	E.
Saturn	887,000,000	F.
Uranus	1,800,000,000	G.
Neptune	2,800,000,000	H.
Pluto (dwarf)	3,600,000,000	I.

Warm-Up 68

What's the Problem?

Work It Out

Jacob listed some very large numbers and scientific and mathematical facts associated with them.

Complete his chart.

Fact	Standard Number	Scientific Notation
Molecules in a drop of water	1,700,000,000,000,000,000,000,000	A. $1.7 \times$
Words printed from 1456 to 1940	10,000,000,000,000,000	B. $1 \times$
Tons of water on Earth	1,410,000,000,000,000,000,000	C. $1.41 \times$
Atoms in a pound of iron	4,891,500,000,000,000,000,000,000	D. $4.8915 \times$
Miles from the Sun to Vega (star)	152,620,000,000,000	E. $1.5262 \times$

Warm-Up 69

What's the Problem?

Work It Out

Joshua needed to find the number closest to zero from a group of numbers. He put these numbers on a number line: -2, 3, 7, -5, 6, -6, -1.

0

1. **Which integer was closest to 0?**

   _____

2. **Which integer had the greatest value?**

   _____

3. **Which integer had the lowest value?**

   _____

Warm-Up 70

What's the Problem?

Work It Out

Joshua needed to find the opposite value of each integer listed below and then place them in order on a number line.

Values: -3, 6, 9, 12, -11, 13, -14, 7, 2, -1, -4

1. **List the opposite value for each integer above in order on the vertical number line.**

2. **Which of the integers from the number line has the greatest value?**

   _____

3. **Which of the integers from the number line has the least value?**

   _____

4. **Which integer is closest to 0?**

   _____

0

Warm-Up 71

What's the Problem?

Sabrina and Jessica were creating a card game with prime and composite numbers using cards numbered from 1 to 25.

Using the numbers 1 through 25, do each of the following on the chart:

- **List all of the prime numbers and all of the composite numbers.**

- **List all of the numbers that are neither prime nor composite.**

- **Circle all of the even prime numbers.**

Work It Out

Prime	Composite	Neither

Warm-Up 72

What's the Problem?

In their card game, Sabrina and Jessica gave 3 points for every odd prime number, 1 point for every composite number, 10 points for every number that is neither prime nor composite, and 10 points for every even prime number.

How many total points are the 25 cards worth?

Work It Out

Warm-Up 73

What's the Problem?

Work It Out

Abigail and Jeanette were looking for a number with the greatest number of factors to use in a computer program. They chose these numbers: 25, 36, 48, 64, 96, and 100.

1. **List all of the factors for each number in the space to the right.**

2. **Which of these numbers has the greatest number of factors?**

_____

Warm-Up 74

What's the Problem?

Work It Out

Abigail and Jeanette wanted to find the greatest common factor of 80 and 120.

1. **List all of the factors for each number in the space to the right.**

2. **What is the greatest common factor?**

_____

Warm-Up 75

What's the Problem?

Work It Out

Justin and Gregory knew that the largest perfect square under 100 was 81, which equaled 9 x 9, or 9 squared. They wanted to find the largest perfect square under 200.

1. How can they find the largest square?

_____

_____

_____

_____

2. What is the largest perfect square under 200?

_____

Warm-Up 76

What's the Problem?

Work It Out

Gregory thought he could find the largest perfect square less than 500 by multiplying numbers larger than 10 by themselves to find the answer.

1. What is the largest perfect square less than 500?

_____

2. Does Gregory's system work?

_____

3. What is the largest perfect square under 1,000?

_____

What's the Problem?

Work It Out

Kari and her mother went shopping for a new dress for the sixth-grade promotion ceremony. Kari found the perfect dress in size and color, but it was expensive at $150. However, there was a sale sign that said all the dresses on that rack were $\frac{1}{2}$ off the regular price. When they took it to the checkout stand, the clerk gave them only $\frac{1}{3}$ off the regular price. It must have been on the wrong rack.

1. **What was the sale price for the dress?**

   _____

2. **How much did they save on the dress?**

   _____

What's the Problem?

Work It Out

When Kari and her mom went shopping for shoes to match Kari's dress, they found a perfect pair in the right size for $120. The sign next to the shoes offered a 1-day special of $\frac{1}{4}$ off the regular price. At the checkout counter, they used a coupon that gave them an additional $\frac{1}{3}$ discount off the sale price.

1. **What was the final sale price for the shoes before tax?**

   _____

2. **How much did she save altogether on the cost of the shoes?**

   _____

Warm-Up 79

What's the Problem?

Work It Out

Doreen and her mom went shopping for a winter outfit for their snow trip. They found a pair of ski pants with a matching sweater that cost $145.75. They were on sale at 40% off. At the checkout stand, the sale price was cut another 30%.

1. **How much did Doreen's mom actually pay for the outfit before tax?**

   _____

2. **How much did they save off the original price?**

   _____

Warm-Up 80

What's the Problem?

Work It Out

Doreen needed new ski boots, and she found just the right pair for $110. The boots were on sale at 25% off. They received an additional 10% off the sale price for paying cash.

1. **How much did she actually pay for the ski boots before tax?**

   _____

2. **How much did she save off the original price?**

   _____

Warm-Up 81

What's the Problem?

Work It Out

Casey played Little League baseball as a center fielder. In his first game he got 4 hits in 6 at bats. He went 1 for 4 in his second game and 2 for 3 in his third game. He got 4 hits in 4 at bats in the fourth game and went 1 for 5 in the fifth game. He wanted to compute his batting average.

1. **How many total hits did he have in the 5 games?**_____

2. **How many total at bats did he have in the 5 games?**_____

3. **What was his batting average when he divided the total at bats into the number of hits? (Remember to carry the division to 3 places after the decimal.)**

_____

Warm-Up 82

What's the Problem?

Work It Out

In the first month of the season, Casey had 38 hits in 84 at bats. In the second month, he collected 40 hits in 91 at bats. He was hoping to have a .400 batting average or better because he wanted to eventually play baseball in high school.

1. **What was Casey's batting average for the first month?**_____

2. **What was Casey's batting average for the second month?**

_____

3. **What was Casey's overall batting average for the 2 months? Use his total hits divided by his total at bats.**

_____

4. **Did he have a .400 batting average or better?**_____

Warm-Up 83

What's the Problem?

Work It Out

Michael and Charles always compare their shooting percentages after each basketball game during the winter league tournament in their community. In the first game of the playoffs, Michael took 25 shots and made 15 field goals. Charles took 40 shots and made 25 field goals.

1. What was Michael's shooting percentage?

_____

2. What was Charles' shooting percentage?

_____

3. Who had the better shooting percentage?

_____

Warm-Up 84

What's the Problem?

Work It Out

In the final game of the basketball tournament, Michael made 28 field goals in 36 shots. Charles made 14 field goals in 18 attempts.

1. What was Michael's shooting percentage?

_____

2. What was Charles' shooting percentage?

_____

3. Who had the better shooting percentage?

_____

What's the Problem?

Work It Out

Marcie is the quarterback on the girls' football team. In her first game, she attempted 22 passes and completed 14 of them.

What was her percentage of completed passes rounded to the tenths place?

_____

- -

What's the Problem?

Work It Out

During the championship game against their cross-town rivals, Marcie attempted 40 passes and completed 31 of them.

What was her completion percentage rounded to the tenths place?

_____

What's the Problem?

Work It Out

Elena was traveling with her parents by car from her home near San Francisco, California, to her uncle's house in Philadelphia, Pennsylvania, a distance of 2,850 miles. They traveled an average of 50 miles per hour.

1. **How many hours of driving did it take Elena to reach her uncle's home?**

   _____

2. **How many hours would it have taken them if they had traveled at 60 miles per hour?**

   _____

3. **How many hours of travel would they have saved?**

   _____

What's the Problem?

Work It Out

When Elena's family left Philadelphia, they drove 1,450 miles to her grandmother's home in Dallas, Texas. They took 40 hours to arrive in Dallas.

1. **How many miles per hour did they average on this trip?**

   _____

2. **How many miles per hour would they have averaged if they took only 30 hours to arrive in Dallas?**

   _____

Warm-Up 89

What's the Problem?

Work It Out

Susie's dad gets 32 miles per gallon driving his new car on the highway. He took the family on a 2,000-mile road trip from Chicago, Illinois, to Los Angeles, California. He paid $3.50 a gallon for gas.

1. **How many gallons did it take to make the trip from Chicago to Los Angeles?**

   _____

2. **How much did it cost for gasoline to make the trip to Los Angeles?**

   _____

- -

Warm-Up 90

What's the Problem?

Work It Out

On the second leg of their road trip, Susie and her family drove 960 miles from Los Angeles, California, to Portland, Oregon. Her dad got 32 miles to the gallon and paid $3.40 a gallon.

1. **How many gallons did it take to make the trip from Los Angeles to Portland?**

   _____

2. **How much did it cost for gasoline to get there?**

   _____

Warm-Up 91

What's the Problem?

Work It Out

Ashley is tired of her plain brown room with dull brown paint. Her mother is going to let her choose hot pink wallpaper with shiny sparkles. But first, she has to compute the area to determine how much wallpaper she needs. Two walls of her room are 10 feet high and 18 feet wide. The other 2 walls are 10 feet high and 22 feet wide.

1. **What is the total area of her walls in square feet?**

   _____

2. **What is the perimeter of her room?**

   _____

Warm-Up 92

What's the Problem?

Work It Out

The wallpaper Ashley wants is sold by the square yard. A square yard is equal to 9 square feet.

How many square yards does Ashley need?

_____

Warm-Up 93

What's the Problem?

Work It Out

Aiden's parents are going to replant their lawn with fresh sod. Their entire lot is 120 feet wide and 90 feet deep. The house is 80 feet long and 60 feet deep. The garage is 40 feet wide and 20 feet deep. Aiden needs to figure how many square feet are not occupied by the house and the garage.

1. What is the area of the lot in square feet?

_____

2. What is the area of the house in square feet?

_____

3. What is the area of the garage in square feet?

_____

4. How many square feet will be covered by the sod to make a new lawn?

_____

. . . .

Warm-Up 94

Work It Out

What's the Problem?

Sod is sold by the square yard. A square yard equals 9 square feet.

1. How many square yards of sod will Aiden's family need for the new lawn?

_____

2. Aiden has to plant flowers along the entire perimeter of the lot. How many feet will Aiden plant in flowers?

_____

Warm-Up 95

What's the Problem?

Work It Out

Joshua has 1,000 building blocks that he uses to design buildings, bridges, and other structures. Each block is exactly 1 inch wide, 1 inch long, and 1 inch high. His mom gave him a box to store his blocks. The box is 12 inches long, 8 inches wide, and 10 inches high.

1. What is the volume of the box?

_____

2. Will all of the blocks fit into the box?

_____

Warm-Up 96

What's the Problem?

Work It Out

Joshua wanted to fit all 1,000 blocks into a large cube that was the same in length, width, and height.

What will the length, width, and height of the cube be?

_____

Geometry: polygons; interior angles

What's the Problem?

Work It Out

Georgia loves geometry. In her geometry class, she drew the following regular (equal-sided) polygons. Georgia used a ruler and a protractor to draw the figures and measure the angles.

Complete the information on the chart.

triangle

square

pentagon

hexagon

octagon

nonagon

decagon

dodecagon

Polygon	# of Sides	Degrees of 1 Interior Angle	Total Degrees
Triangle			
Square			
Pentagon			
Hexagon			
Octagon			
Nonagon			
Decagon			
Dodecagon			

What's the Problem?

Work It Out

Georgia's geometry teacher asked her the following questions after he saw her completed chart.

1. **Which figure has the largest interior angle?**

   _____

2. **Which figure has the largest number of degrees in all interior angles?**

   _____

triangle

square

pentagon

hexagon

octagon

nonagon

decagon

dodecagon

Geometry: triangles

What's the Problem?

Work It Out

Annissa has an area of dirt behind her house shaped like this quadrilateral:

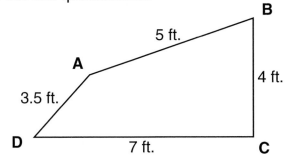

She is going to divide the area into 2 triangular sections. Triangle ABC will be planted with sunflowers, Annissa's favorite flower. Triangle ACD will be planted with tulips, her mother's favorite flower. The length of side AB is exactly the same length as from point A to point C.

What is the perimeter of each flowerbed?

_____

· ·

What's the Problem?

Work It Out

Anissa drew 2 triangles. The height of triangle A is 3.5 ft. The base of triangle A is 5 ft. The height of triangle B is 5 ft. The base of triangle B is 4.5 ft.

What is the area of each triangle?

_____

_____

What's the Problem?

Leonardo's mother bought a pepperoni pizza for Leonardo and his twin brother, Raphael. They always order pizza from a place that makes rectangular pizzas. The pizza was exactly 16 inches long and 6 inches wide. Because the boys were always squabbling over who got more, she cut the pizza in half from point A to point C.

Work It Out

How many square inches of pizza did each brother receive?

_____

What's the Problem?

If Leonardo got 1 serving of food, his twin brother, Raphael, always wanted 2 servings. Their mother wanted to be completely fair and equal in the amount of dessert each brother got for a birthday party. She made a tray of fudge that was 6 inches long and 3 inches wide. She used a knife to cut the fudge into 3 triangular pieces with just 2 straight lines.

Draw lines to show where their mother can make the 2 straight cuts so that Leonardo gets half of the fudge in 1 piece and Raphael gets 2 pieces that equal only half of the fudge.

Work It Out

Geometry: volume

What's the Problem?

Work It Out

Joseph has a set of 12 colorful and exciting science fiction paperback books. Each book is 9 inches long, 6 inches wide, and 1 inch thick.

Which of the following boxes would be best to use to store his books without damaging the books or having a lot of extra space left over?

Box A: 12 inches long, 15 inches wide, 5 inches high

Box B: 12 inches long, 7 inches wide, 10 inches high

Box C: 6 inches long, 12 inches wide, 6 inches high

Box D: 10 inches long, 6 inches wide, 12 inches high

- -

What's the Problem?

Work It Out

Joseph has a set of 144 wooden cubes for a game. Each cube is 1 inch long, 1 inch wide, and 1 inch high. He wants to store them in the smallest box that will hold all 144 cubes.

Which of the following boxes will hold all of the cubes in the smallest possible space?

Box A: 12 inches long by 12 inches wide by 12 inches high

Box B: 6 inches long by 6 inches wide by 6 inches high

Box C: 6 inches long by 6 inches wide by 4 inches high

Box D: 12 inches long by 12 inches wide by 4 inches wide

What's the Problem?

Work It Out

Irene is making a large chocolate cream pie for her friends who are coming to dinner. The distance from the outer edge of the pie to the exact center of the pie is 6 inches.

1. What is the circumference of the pie?

_____

2. What is the area the pie will cover?

_____

What's the Problem?

Work It Out

Irene's aunt made her a very large pie to share with her family. The distance from the outer edge of the pie to the exact center of the pie is 10 inches.

1. What is the circumference of the pie?

_____

2. What is the area the pie will cover?

_____

Warm-Up 107

What's the Problem?   Work It Out

Audrey's mother works in a bakery. She makes banana cream pies in tins. Each tin has a radius of 9 inches.

1. **What is the circumference of each pie?**

   _____

2. **What is the area of each pie?**

   _____

- -

Warm-Up 108

What's the Problem?   Work It Out

Audrey's mother packs pies in circular boxes. Each box has a radius of 10 inches and is 2 inches high.

What is the volume of a cylinder that will hold 10 of these boxed pies?

(Volume of a cylinder = $\pi r^2 \times h$)

_____

What's the Problem?

Work It Out

Jessica's older brother gave her an ugly, old wooden box to hold her dolls. Jessica decided to cover the box with bright red foil with shiny, embossed stars. The box was 12 inches wide, 12 inches long, and 12 inches high.

How many square inches of foil did Jessica need to cover all 6 sides of the box?

_____

What's the Problem?

Work It Out

Jessica liked her colorful box so much that she decided to cover an old wooden trunk where she kept her board games, skates, and scooter to match. The trunk was 5 feet long, 3 feet wide, and 2.5 feet high.

How many square feet of red foil will Jessica need to cover the 4 sides and top of the trunk?

_____

Geometry: volume; area

What's the Problem?

Work It Out

Jerry's dad wants to replant their front lawn with a covering of good, new soil. He wants to spread the soil 3 inches ($\frac{1}{4}$ of a foot) deep over an area that is 40 feet wide and 60 feet long.

How many cubic feet of soil will he need to use?

_____

What's the Problem?

Work It Out

Jerry's neighbor is going to cover his entire lawn with new grass sod. One part of his lawn is 90 feet long and 40 feet wide. The second section is 30 feet long and 20 feet wide. Grass sod is sold by the square yard.

1. **How many square feet of lawn does Jerry's neighbor need to cover?**

   _____

2. **How many square yards of sod does he need?**

   _____

Warm-Up 113

What's the Problem?

Work It Out

Alex drew a map of his neighborhood using a coordinate plane to locate the important features. The location of each feature can be identified by the ordered pairs on the graph.

Study the coordinate plane and name the location of each feature using the ordered pairs.

Alex's home = _____

Grocery store = _____

Pizza parlor = _____

School = _____

Small farm = _____

Convenience store = _____

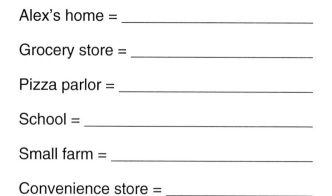

- -

Warm-Up 114

What's the Problem?

Work It Out

Which feature is located at each of these sets of ordered pairs on Alex's map?

(4, 7) _____

(6, 1) _____

(15, 10) _____

(3, 10) _____

(10, 3) _____

(3, 2) _____

(13, 5) _____

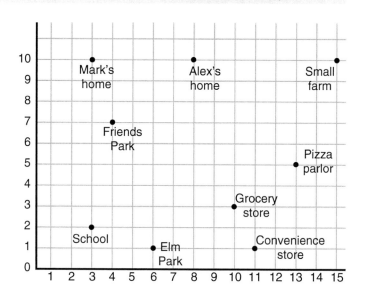

Geometry: coordinate plane

What's the Problem?

Work It Out

Allison had to babysit her little brother, Jason, and his friend Justin, while their mothers went shopping. She decided to hide treasures for the boys to find—but they had to be able to understand the map she made for them.

What did she hide for the boys at each of these coordinate pairs?

(15, 1) _____

(2, 13) _____

(12, 7) _____

(8, 3) _____

(5, 9) _____

(15, 15) _____

(11, 13) _____

(8, 5) _____

(10, 10) _____

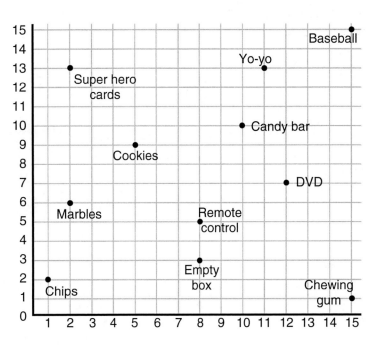

What's the Problem?

Work It Out

What are the coordinates for these prizes on the map?

Marbles _____

Cookies _____

DVD _____

Chewing gum _____

Candy bar _____

Chips _____

Baseball _____

Yo-yo _____

Geometry: coordinate plane/4 quadrants

What's the Problem?

Work It Out

Charlene made a map on a coordinate plane to show where all of her best friends' seats in the classroom were compared to hers, which was exactly in the middle of the classroom at point (0, 0).

Identify the friend's name and the quadrant at each pair of coordinates listed below.

Coordinates	Name	Quadrant
(9, -3)		
(9, 7)		
(-6, -6)		
(-4, -3)		
(-4, 4)		
(6, -6)		
(-6, 6)		
(3, 4)		

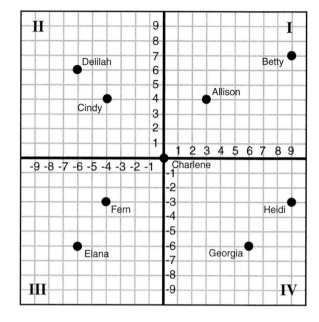

What's the Problem?

Work It Out

At what coordinates do each of these friends sit?

Name	Coordinates
Charlene	(0, 0)
Allison	
Betty	
Cindy	
Delilah	
Elana	
Fern	
Georgia	
Heidi	

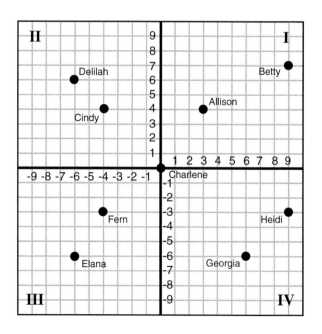

Warm-Up 119

What's the Problem?

Jodelle found this mysterious, crumpled map lying partially hidden under her brother's pillow when she was helping her mother straighten the house and do the daily chores. She quickly realized that the big pine tree in the yard was the central point and she saw fresh digging at points corresponding to the dots on the map. Her brother had listed what he had buried.

Name the coordinates that correspond to each buried item.

Buried Treasure	Coordinates
Jodelle's dolls	
Coins	
Secret #1	
Secret #2	
Candy	
Paper money	
Cards	
Marbles	

Work It Out

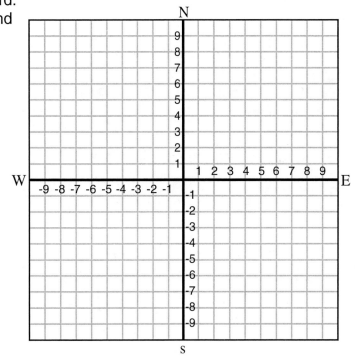

Warm-Up 120

What's the Problem?

Jodelle buried different items in her backyard. She made a list so that her brother could find the items.

Label the locations on the map where she buried her secret treasures.

(8, -8)   her picture

(-8, -8)   a fashion magazine

(-8, 8)   3 pennies

(8, 8)   newspapers

(4, 4)   plastic soldiers

(-4, -4)   times table cards

(4, -4)   sour candy balls

(-4, 4)   a bag of small pebbles

Work It Out

Warm-Up 121

What's the Problem?

Work It Out

Kevin drew a very accurate map of three roads he traveled on as he rode his bicycle to school. He measured the distance between Park Lane and Franklin Street with a yardstick. He found that they were consistently exactly the same distance apart and were therefore parallel streets. Elm Avenue was a straight road that crossed Park Lane and Franklin Street making a 60-degree angle at angle 1.

What are the angle measurements for the angles shown in the map?

_____

_____

_____

_____

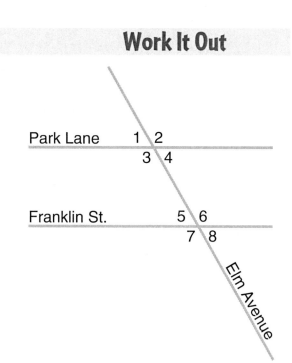

- -

Warm-Up 122

What's the Problem?

Work It Out

1. **Which angles are equal to each other?**

   _____

   _____

2. **What do angles 1 and 2 equal together?**

   _____

3. **Which angles are supplementary angles?**

   _____

   _____

4. **Which angles are opposite?**

   _____

   _____

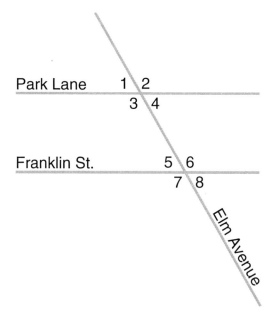

Warm-Up 123

What's the Problem?

Sabrina helped her mother slice a freshly baked pizza for her and her siblings. She intended to give the smallest pieces to her little brothers and the largest pieces to her parents. She and her sister would have the medium slices. Sabrina made 3 straight cuts with the pizza roller. Section B is 40 degrees. Section F is 60 degrees.

1. How many degrees are in the entire circle?

   _____

2. How many degrees are in each section?

   _____

   _____

   _____

3. Who ate what slice? _____

   _____

Work It Out

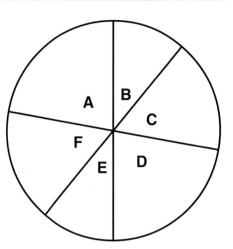

• •

Warm-Up 124

What's the Problem?

When Sabrina cut an apple pie for the family, she cut 9 pieces. She cut 3 equal pieces, which together were half of the pie. The other half of the pie she cut into 6 equal pieces.

1. How many degrees were
   in the entire circular pie? _____

2. How many degrees were in each of the
   3 larger pieces?

   _____

3. How many degrees were in each of the
   smaller pieces?

   _____

4. How many smaller pieces would equal
   1 larger piece?

   _____

Work It Out

Warm-Up 125

What's the Problem?

Work It Out

Marlene quizzed her brother: "I am a triangle with 2 equal angles and 1 right angle. What is my name? How many degrees are in each angle? What shapes can be made with 2 of me?"

Answer Marlene's questions.

_____

_____

_____

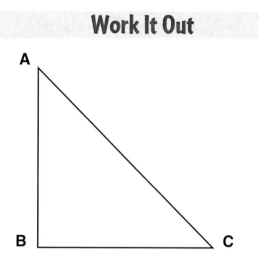

Warm-Up 126

What's the Problem?

Work It Out

Marlene's brother quizzed her: "I am a triangle with 2 equal sides. One angle equals 120 degrees. What is my name? How many degrees are in each angle? What shape can be made with 3 of me?"

Answer Marlene's brother's questions.

_____

_____

_____

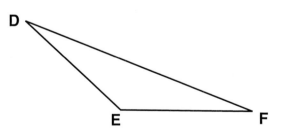

Warm-Up 127

What's the Problem?

Work It Out

Jessica and Valerie decided to fill a round brick planter in their backyard with dirt and plant flower seeds. They measured the diameter across the center of the circular planter. It was 36 inches. The height of the planter was 24 inches.

1. **What was the radius of the planter?**

   _____

2. **How many square inches of space at the top of the planter could they use to spread flower seeds?**

   _____

3. **How many cubic inches of dirt did they need to fill the cylinder with soil?**

   (Volume of a cylinder = $\pi r^2 \times h$)

   _____

• •

Warm-Up 128

What's the Problem?

Work It Out

The girls decided to put a thin ribbon of bright pink plastic around the edge of the planter.

What was the distance around, or the circumference, of the planter?

_____

Warm-Up 129

What's the Problem?

William was using dominoes to make model figures. He placed 3 dominoes in a row along 1 side of a triangle and 5 dominoes in a row along the hypotenuse (the long side of the triangle).

How many dominoes will he need to make the other side?

_____

Work It Out

Pythagorean theorem: $a^2 + b^2 = c^2$

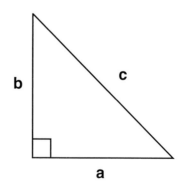

Warm-Up 130

What's the Problem?

In making his second triangle, William placed 12 dominoes along 1 side of the triangle and 5 dominoes along the other side of the triangle.

How many dominoes will he need for the hypotenuse of this triangle?

_____

Work It Out

Pythagorean theorem: $a^2 + b^2 = c^2$

Warm-Up 131

What's the Problem? **Work It Out**

Misty knew that a penny is about 1.5 millimeters thick. She carefully stacked clean, undamaged pennies until she had a pile about 1 centimeter tall.

1. **How many pennies did she get to approximately equal 1 centimeter in height?**

   _____

2. **How many pennies would it take to make a pile approximately 10 centimeters tall?**

   _____

3. **A meter is 100 centimeters. How many pennies would approximately equal 1 meter tall?**

   _____

- -

Warm-Up 132

What's the Problem? **Work It Out**

Misty knew that a penny is about 1.5 millimeters thick. She carefully stacked undamaged pennies until she had a pile 1 inch tall. She also knew that it takes about $2\frac{1}{2}$ centimeters to equal 1 inch.

1. **How many pennies do you think it would take to approximately make a 1-inch stack?**

   _____

2. **Approximately how many pennies would a 12-inch ruler measure?**

   _____

3. **Approximately how many pennies would a yardstick (36 inches) measure?**

   _____

Warm-Up 133

What's the Problem?   **Work It Out**

Kimberly was given a photo of her best friend, Heather, that was exactly 7 inches long and 5 inches wide. She needed to buy a rectangular picture frame that was 1 inch longer on all sides to hold the photo without cutting off any part of the picture.

1. **How big does the picture frame need to be?**_____

2. **What is the area of the photo?**_____

3. **What is the perimeter of the photo?**_____

4. **What is the area of the picture frame?**_____

5. **What is the perimeter of the picture frame?**_____

Warm-Up 134

What's the Problem?   **Work It Out**

Kimberly has a mirror over her dresser that has 4 photos stuck over the glass. The mirror is 16 inches wide and 20 inches long. The first photo of her brother is 6 inches long and 4 inches wide. The photo of her 3 friends from kindergarten is 4 inches long and 4 inches wide. The photo of Kimberly and her mother is 6 inches long and 6 inches wide. The photo of her dad is 4 inches long and 3 inches wide.

1. **What is the area of the entire mirror?** _____

2. **What is the area of each photo?**

   _____

   _____

3. **How many square inches of the mirror are not covered by photos?**

   _____

Warm-Up 135

What's the Problem?   Work It Out

Aaron is a gifted artist. His father offered to take him to his favorite fast-food place if he could draw 3 triangles on a large piece of construction paper of exactly these lengths. The first triangle had to be 4 inches on one side and exactly 2 inches on each of the other two sides. The second triangle had to be 6 inches long on one side and exactly 3 inches long on the other two sides. The third triangle had to be 5 inches long on the long side, 2 inches long on a second side, and exactly 3 inches long on the third side.

1. **Draw each of these triangles on the back or front of this paper.**

2. **Describe your results.**

_____

_____

_____

_____

Warm-Up 136

What's the Problem?   Work It Out

Aaron offered to draw the following triangles for his father. The first would be 4 inches long on one side and 3 inches long on the other two sides. The second would be 6 inches long on one side and $3\frac{1}{2}$ inches long on the other two sides. The third would be 5 inches long on one side and 3 inches long on the other two sides.

1. **Draw each of these triangles on paper.**

2. **Describe your results.**

_____

_____

_____

3. **Why were you able to draw these triangles?**

_____

_____

Warm-Up 137

What's the Problem?

Kathy and her sister, Molly, wanted to plant a lawn with an edge of flowers in an empty piece of land near their garage. They sketched the shape of the lawn.

1. **What is the area of the rectangular section?** _____

2. **What is the area of the triangular section?** _____

3. **How many square feet of soil do they have to plant grass seed in?**

   _____

4. **A 1-pound box of the grass seed they're using will cover an area of 20 square feet. How many boxes of grass seed do they need to buy?**

   _____

Work It Out

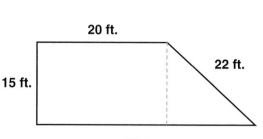

Warm-Up 138

What's the Problem?

Kathy and Molly wanted to plant a border of flowers along the entire outer edge of the lawn. They sketched the shape of the lawn.

1. **How many feet of flowers will they plant?**

   _____

2. **If 5 flower seedlings can be planted along each foot, how many seedlings will they need for the entire perimeter of the lawn?**

   _____

Work It Out

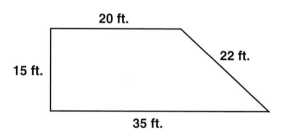

Warm-Up 139

What's the Problem?   **Work It Out**

Margaret and Nancy share a room. Margaret wants to cover the door of her closet with a shiny poster of her favorite movie star and Molly wants to put up a poster of her favorite female soccer player. Their mother told them to divide the door into 2 equal right triangles. The closet door is 4 feet wide and 8 feet high.

1. **What is the total area of the closet door?**

   _____

2. **What is the area of each right triangle?**

   _____

- -

Warm-Up 140

What's the Problem?   **Work It Out**

When they were picking out new carpeting for their room, Molly wanted bright purple and Margaret wanted lemon-yellow carpet. Their mother had them divide the room into 2 right triangles. The length of the room was 20 feet and the width was 18 feet.

1. **What was the area of the floor?**

   _____

2. **What was the area of each piece of carpet for the girls?**

   _____

3. **The longest side of each triangle was 27 feet. What was the perimeter of each right triangle?**

   _____

Warm-Up 141

What's the Problem?

The blacktop playground at Sunnyvale School is shaped like a parallelogram. Kelly and Jason measured the blacktop. The long side of the parallelogram was 300 feet. The short side was 140 feet. The distance from A to E shown on the figure was 100 feet.

1. **What is the perimeter of the parallelogram?**

   _____

2. **What is the area of the parallelogram?**

   _____

Work It Out

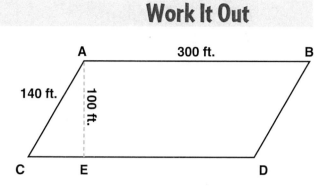

- -

Warm-Up 142

What's the Problem?

Kelly and Jason measured the distance around the school property, which was shaped like a parallelogram. The distances are recorded on their drawing.

1. **What is the perimeter of the entire parallelogram?**

   _____

2. **What is the area of the entire parallelogram?**

   _____

Work It Out

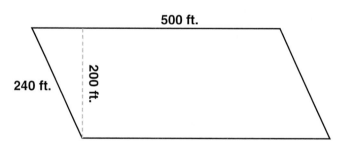

Warm-Up 143

What's the Problem?

Work It Out

Jonathan and Johnny made a simple equal arm balance using a ruler. Johnny balanced the ruler on his finger at a point exactly half the length of the ruler at the 6-inch mark. Jonathan placed a large pink eraser at one end of the ruler. Johnny held the eraser in place with a finger while Jonathan carefully placed pennies on the other end of the ruler until the ruler balanced evenly with the eraser on one end and the pennies on the other end. A penny and a large paper clip each weigh about 1 gram.

Do the experiment above using pennies or by sliding large paper clips on the end of the ruler to find out how many grams each of the objects in the table weigh. Add 2 more objects of your choice.

Object	Grams
Pencil	
Eraser	
Marker	
Crayon	
Quarter	
Pebble	
_____	
_____	

Warm-Up 144

What's the Problem?

Work It Out

Johnny and Jonathan used a scale with ounces and pounds marked to weigh science specimens and materials in the classroom. An ounce weighs about 28 grams.

Convert these ounces to grams in the chart.

Science Specimen	Ounces	Grams
Large cone	0.5	
Deer bone	4	
Antlers	7	
Scallop shell	0.75	
Abalone shell	2	
Shell guide	4	
Field guide	12	

Warm-Up 145

What's the Problem?

Work It Out

Barbara bought a 1-pound box (16 ounces) of modeling clay for a science project. The clay was wrapped in 4 equal plastic packages. Barbara used 1 of the 4 packages to make a model sea lion. She used 1.5 packages to mold a model dolphin, and half a package for the dolphin's young calf. She molded 3 sea otters from the remaining package.

1. **How many ounces each did she use to mold the sea lion, the dolphin, the calf, and 1 sea otter?**

   _____

   _____

2. **How many grams did each sea animal mold equal?**

   _____

   _____

Warm-Up 146

What's the Problem?

Work It Out

Craig bought a 1-pound box (16 ounces) of modeling clay to make model sharks. The clay was packaged in 4 equal plastic covered packages. He used 1 of the 4 packages to mold a hammerhead shark. He used $1\frac{1}{3}$ packages to mold a megamouth shark. He used $1\frac{2}{3}$ of a package to make a great white shark.

1. **How many ounces did he use to mold each shark?**

   _____

   _____

2. **How many grams did each shark mold equal?**

   _____

   _____

Warm-Up 147

What's the Problem?

Work It Out

Casey was watching batting practice with his baseball team and thinking about angles and baseball. His teammate, Tommy, hit a low line drive that went into foul territory. The team's best player, Owen, hit a line drive right over second base. Casey hit a fair ball just inside the first base line. Ivan hit a ball just off the first base line in foul territory. Jorge hit a ball just inside third and down the line.

Identify the angles formed by the named lines as acute or obtuse.

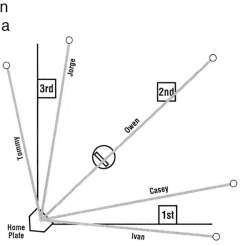

1. **Jorge's hit and 1st base line** _____

2. **Ivan's hit and 3rd base line** _____

3. **Owen's and Casey's hits** _____

4. **Casey's hit and 3rd base line** _____

5. **Ivan's and Owen's hits** _____

6. **Tommy's and Ivan's hits** _____

. . . .

Warm-Up 148

What's the Problem?

Work It Out

Use the diagram to help you answer the following questions.

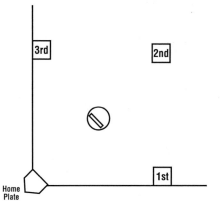

1. **What kind of angle is formed by the lines from home plate to 3rd base and home plate to 1st base? How many degrees are formed inside this angle?**

   _____

2. **What kind of angle is formed outside those same lines in question 1? How many degrees are formed in this outside angle?**

   _____

3. **What kind of angle is formed by a batted ball that hits the pitcher's mound and bounces between 3rd base and 2nd base?**

   _____

What's the Problem?

Work It Out

Mariah has 300 small cubes. Each cube is
1 centimeter long, 1 centimeter wide, and
1 centimeter high. She wants to keep all of the
cubes in 1 box so they don't get lost. She has
3 choices. Her green box is 10 centimeters
long, 3 centimeters wide, and 2 centimeters high.
Her yellow box is 5 centimeters long, 5 centimeters
wide, and 5 centimeters high. Her blue box is
7 centimeters long, 7 centimeters wide, and
7 centimeters high.

Which box will hold all of the cubes? Why?

_____

_____

- -

Warm-Up 150

What's the Problem?

Work It Out

Mariah has 300 small cubes. Each cube's sides
are 1 centimeter in length. She would like a box
in which the cubes fit exactly with none left over
and no extra room.

Compute the size of a box that would work.

_____

What's the Problem?
Work It Out

Jonathan and his math partner, Duane, took each other's pulse 3 times. Jonathan had an average heartbeat of 72 beats per minute. Duane had an average heartbeat of 76 beats per minute.

1. **About how many times will Jonathan's heart beat in 1 hour?**

   _____

2. **About how many times will his heart beat in 1 day?** _____

3. **About how many times will Duane's heart beat in 1 hour?**

   _____

4. **About how many times will Duane's heart beat in 1 day?**

   _____

• •

Warm-Up 152

What's the Problem?
Work It Out

Jonathan's sister, Margaret, and her best friend, Kathy, took each other's pulse 3 times. Margaret had an average heartbeat of 80 beats per minute. Kathy had an average heartbeat of 84 beats per minute.

1. **About how many times will Margaret's heart beat in 1 hour?** _____

2. **About how many times will her heart beat in 1 day?**

   _____

3. **About how many times will Kathy's heart beat in 1 hour?**

   _____

4. **About how many times will Kathy's heart beat in 1 day?**

   _____

What's the Problem?

Work It Out

Kenneth started school on September 1st. He was one of 22 eleven-year-olds in his class. On his next birthday, he wants to join a baseball league for students who are 12 years old. His birthday is on February 23.

Not counting the first day of school, how many more days does he have to wait before he can join the league?

_____

Warm-Up 154

What's the Problem?

Work It Out

Tony was 11 years old when he started school on the first of September. He wants to join the Tigers baseball league, but it's only for kids who are 12 to 13 years old. Tony's birthday is on June 17.

Not counting the first day of school, how many more days does Tony have to wait before he can sign up for the league? (It is not a leap year.)

_____

Warm-Up 155

What's the Problem?   Work It Out

Maureen measured the temperature at noon with a thermometer. It read exactly 96 degrees Fahrenheit. The temperature at 5 P.M. read 69 degrees. At 8 P.M. it was 57 degrees. At midnight, it was 39 degrees.

1. **How much cooler was it at 5 P.M. than at noon?**

   _____

2. **How much cooler was it at 8 P.M. than at noon?**

   _____

3. **How much cooler was it at midnight than at noon?**

   _____

Warm-Up 156

What's the Problem?   Work It Out

During a January blizzard, Maureen measured the temperature at noon, which was 32 degrees Fahrenheit, the freezing point of water. At 5 P.M., the temperature had dropped to 5 degrees above zero. By 9 P.M., the thermometer read 13 degrees below zero. At midnight, the temperature reading was -22 degrees.

1. **How much colder was it at 5 P.M. than at noon?**

   _____

2. **How much colder was it at 9 P.M. than at noon?**

   _____

3. **How much colder was it at midnight than at noon?**

   _____

What's the Problem?

Work It Out

Erica learned that the boiling point of water on the Celsius thermometer is 100 degrees. The boiling point of water on the Fahrenheit scale is 212 degrees. The freezing point of water on the Celsius thermometer is 0 degrees, and 32 degrees on the Fahrenheit scale.

1. **Which temperature scale would be hotter with a reading of 200 degrees?**

   _____

2. **Which temperature scale would be warmer with a reading of 50 degrees below 0?**

   _____

Warm-Up 158

What's the Problem?

Work It Out

Erica read that the temperature on the surface of Venus is over 800° Fahrenheit. The hottest recorded temperature on Earth was 136°F in 1936 in a Libyan desert. The coldest recorded temperature on Earth was -129°F in Antarctica.

1. **How many degrees hotter is the temperature on Venus than the temperature needed to boil water on Earth?**

   _____

2. **How many degrees hotter is the temperature on Venus than the point at which water freezes on Earth?**

   _____

3. **How many degrees hotter is the temperature on Venus than the hottest temperature ever recorded on Earth?**

   _____

What's the Problem?

Work It Out

Annalee measured the radius of a circle. She knows that the formula for the circumference of a circle (the distance around the circle) is C = 2πr, which means the radius is multiplied by 2 and then by π, which is valued at 3.14. The radius is 1 inch.

What is the circumference of the circle?

_____

What's the Problem?

Work It Out

Annalee measured the radius of her favorite music CD at 6 centimeters.

What is the circumference of the CD?

_____

Warm-Up 161

What's the Problem?

Work It Out

Courtney's mother wanted her to plant a round area of soil with grass sod. She also wanted a border of flowers planted around the edge of the circle. Courtney measured the diameter of the round area and found that it was 10 feet long.

1. **What is the radius of the circle?**

   _____

2. **How many square feet of sod will Courtney need to plant the patch of ground?**

   _____

3. **What is the circumference of the circle, which Courtney is going to plant with flowers?**

   _____

Warm-Up 162

What's the Problem?

Work It Out

When her neighbor saw the wonderful job Courtney did on her mother's lawn, she hired Courtney to plant a round area on his property that had a diameter of 15 feet. He wanted sod in the middle and tall flowers along the outer edge.

1. **What is the radius of the circle?**

   _____

2. **How many square feet of sod will Courtney need to plant this patch of ground?**

   _____

3. **What is the circumference of the circle, which Courtney is going to plant with flowers?**

   _____

What's the Problem?   **Work It Out**

Melanie was doing a science project in which she added vinegar to water. She had a small cylinder full of water that had a radius of 1 inch and a height of 4 inches. She had a cylinder full of vinegar that had a radius of 0.5 inches and a height of 3 inches. She was pouring the 2 liquids into an empty cylinder that had a radius of 1 inch and a height of 6 inches.

1. How many cubic inches of water did she use?

_____

2. How many cubic inches of vinegar did she use?

_____

3. Will the empty cylinder hold both the vinegar and water together?

_____

- -

Warm-Up
164

What's the Problem?   **Work It Out**

Melanie needs a cylinder that will hold 50 cubic inches of fluid for an experiment. The cylinder she has at home has a radius of 2 inches and is 4 inches high.

1. How many cubic inches will the cylinder hold?

_____

2. Is the cylinder large enough to hold 50 cubic inches of fluid?

_____

Measurement: volume of a rectangular prism

What's the Problem?

Work It Out

Andy's dad wants him to store 600 decorative bricks in a wooden crate until he is ready to use them. Each brick is 8 inches long, 3 inches wide, and 2 inches high. The crate is 8 feet long, 4 feet wide, and 3 feet high.

1. What is the volume of the crate in cubic feet?

_____

2. What is the volume of the crate in cubic inches?

_____

3. What is the volume of each brick in cubic inches?

_____

4. How many bricks will fit into the crate?

_____

5. Is there enough room for all 600 bricks?

_____

What's the Problem?

Work It Out

The hardware store where Andy's dad shops is having a sale on bricks. Each brick is 8 inches long, 3 inches wide, and 2 inches high. He needs 4,500 bricks to build a special project, and he plans on storing the bricks in a crate that is 10 feet long, 6 feet wide, and 2 feet high.

1. What is the volume of this crate in cubic feet?

_____

2. What is the volume of this crate in cubic inches?

_____

3. What is the volume of each brick in cubic inches?

_____

4. How many bricks will fit into the crate?

_____

5. Is there enough room for all the bricks for the special project? _____

Warm-Up 167

What's the Problem?　　　　　　　Work It Out

One storage shed at the local park where Jessica and Kristin play is shaped like a triangular prism. The base is 4 feet wide and 9 feet long and the height is 10 feet. The girls decided to determine how many cubic feet of storage space the building would hold. They knew that the volume of a triangular prism is half that of a rectangular prism.

1. If the building was a rectangular prism with the same base and height, how many cubic feet of storage would it hold?

_____

2. What is the cubic footage of the storage shed?

_____

Warm-Up 168

What's the Problem?　　　　　　　Work It Out

Jessica and Kristin saw a large shed in the shape of a triangular prism at a neighbor's house. It was 8 feet wide, 12 feet high, and 12 feet long. They knew that the volume of a triangular prism is half that of a rectangular prism.

1. If this building was a rectangular prism with the same base and height, how many cubic feet of storage would it hold?

_____

2. What is the cubic footage of the storage shed?

_____

What's the Problem?

Work It Out

Jamal helped his younger brother, James, build a club house in their backyard so that James would have a place to play with his friends. It was in the shape of a square pyramid. The base of the building was 12 feet wide and 12 feet long. The building was 8 feet high. Jamal wanted to determine how many cubic feet of space was inside the pyramid.

What is the volume of the pyramid?

Volume of a pyramid = (Area of base x height) ÷ 3

_____

What's the Problem?

Work It Out

The new play structure at the park was in the shape of a rectangular pyramid. Jamal loved playing inside it with his friends. The pyramid was 14 feet long and 18 feet wide. The height was 10 feet.

What is the volume of the pyramid?

Volume of a pyramid = (Area of base x height) ÷ 3

_____

Warm-Up 171

What's the Problem?

Marlene recorded the number of students who were driven to school by parents, those who came by bus, and those who walked or bicycled to school. She recorded information for early arrivals and those who came just before school started at 8:00 A.M. Each tally mark on her chart represents 1 student. Marlene remembered to include herself in the tally.

How many students . . .

1. were driven to school early by parents? _____

2. were driving by parents in the last 15 minutes? _____

3. walked to school or rode bikes that day? _____

4. attended school that day? _____

5. How many more students rode the later bus than the early bus? _____

Work It Out

	7:30 – 7:45	7:46 – 8:00
Driven by Parents	卌 卌 卌 卌 卌 卌 卌 卌 卌 卌 卌 卌 卌 卌 卌 卌 卌 II	卌 III
Rode the Bus	卌 卌 卌 卌 卌 III	卌 卌 卌 卌 卌 卌 卌 I
Walked or Biked	卌 卌 卌 卌 卌 卌 卌 卌 I	卌 卌 卌 卌 卌 I

- -

Warm-Up 172

What's the Problem?

Marlene's tally chart shows the number of students who were driven to school by parents, those who came by bus, and those who walked or bicycled to school. Each tally mark represents 1 student.

What percentage of the students . . .

1. arrived 15 minutes or more early?_____

2. arrived in the last 15 minutes? _____

3. were driven by their parents? _____

4. arrived by bus? _____

5. walked or rode bikes? _____

Work It Out

	7:30 – 7:45	7:46 – 8:00
Driven by Parents	卌 卌 卌 卌 卌 卌 卌 卌 卌 卌 卌 卌 卌 卌 卌 卌 卌 II	卌 III
Rode the Bus	卌 卌 卌 卌 卌 III	卌 卌 卌 卌 卌 卌 卌 I
Walked or Biked	卌 卌 卌 卌 卌 卌 卌 卌 I	卌 卌 卌 卌 卌 I

Warm-Up 173

What's the Problem?

Megan and Jonathan surveyed the foods chosen by the sixth graders in the school cafeteria. They recorded the foods bought from the cafeteria and those who brought their lunch and recorded the data on the tally chart.

How many students . . .

1. chose corn dogs? _____

2. chose hot dogs? _____

3. chose a veggie plate? _____

4. brought their lunches? _____

5. were surveyed? _____

Work It Out

Corn Dogs
⊮ ⊮ ⊮ ⊮ I

Hot Dogs
⊮ ⊮ ⊮ ⊮ ⊮ II

Veggie Plate
⊮ II

Brought Lunch
⊮ ⊮ ⊮ III

- -

Warm-Up 174

What's the Problem?

Megan and Jonathan's tally chart shows the number of students who bought food from the cafeteria and those who brought their lunches from home.

What percentage of the students . . .

1. brought lunch from home? _____

2. bought corn dogs? _____

3. bought hot dogs? _____

4. bought a veggie plate? _____

5. How would the people running the school cafeteria use this data?

_____

Work It Out

Corn Dogs
⊮ ⊮ ⊮ ⊮ I

Hot Dogs
⊮ ⊮ ⊮ ⊮ ⊮ II

Veggie Plate
⊮ II

Brought Lunch
⊮ ⊮ ⊮ III

6. What data from this chart might be useful to parents?

_____

**Warm-Up
175**

What's the Problem?   Work It Out

During a science project to discover how well water sticks to itself, students were using an eyedropper to place drops on a penny until the water spilled over. Mark got 61 drops on his penny. Andrew got 57 drops on his penny. Alex had 49 drops and Alicia got 53 drops on hers before the water spilled. Jamie got 59 drops and Michelle put 47 on hers. Olivia got 79 drops on her penny.

1. **Place the numbers in order from least to greatest.**

   _____

2. **Compute the range of these numbers by subtracting the least value from the greatest.**

   _____

3. **What is the mode, the most frequently occurring number?** _____

4. **What is the median number in the middle of this group of numbers?** _____

5. **What is the mean, the average of these numbers?** _____

- -

**Warm-Up
176**

What's the Problem?   Work It Out

After doing a science experiment to see how many drops of water will fit on a penny without spilling over, these 7 students recorded their data in a chart.

Name	Number of Drops
Cory	88
Adam	78
Phillip	51
Alan	70
Marie	70
Michael	52
Sophia	67

1. **Place the numbers in order from least to greatest.**

   _____

2. **Compute the range of these numbers by subtracting the least value from the greatest.**

   _____

3. **What is the mode, the most frequently occurring number?** _____

4. **What is the median number in the middle of this group of numbers?** _____

5. **What is the mean, the average of these numbers?** _____

Warm-Up 177

What's the Problem?

Work It Out

Gavin and Lenny were organizing change after an ice cream fundraiser for their class at school. They had stacks of dimes with the following number of coins in each one: 17, 15, 22, 19, 25, 19, and 16.

1. What is the range of these numbers?

_____

2. What is the mode of these numbers?

_____

3. What is the median?

_____

4. What is the mean?

_____

Warm-Up 178

What's the Problem?

Work It Out

Lenny has 7 piles of dimes with the following number of dimes in each one: 16, 19, 21, 20, 14, 16, and 13. He wanted to rearrange the piles so they would all be the same height with the same number of dimes.

1. How many dimes would be in each pile?

_____

2. Which of the measures of central tendency did he find when all of the piles had an equal number of pennies?

_____

Warm-Up 179

What's the Problem?

Anthony and Antonia compiled data on the value of coins in 8 of their classmates' pockets. They compiled the data in an organized list.

1. What is the range of the values?

   _____

2. What is the mode?

   _____

3. What is the median? (Average the 2 middle numbers.)

   _____

4. What is the mean?

   _____

Work It Out

Minnie	$0.88
Max	$0.35
Gary	$0.44
Freddie	$0.19
Ava	$0.51
Ginny	$0.95
Maria	$0.43
Linda	$0.27

Warm-Up 180

What's the Problem?

1. Using the data above, how much money would you be likely to find in the pockets of a student in this room? Explain your answer.

   _____

   _____

   _____

2. Which measure of central tendency—mode, median, or mean—is the most likely to be useful in determining the best numbers to use for noting trends and evaluating your data?

   _____

3. How do you find the median in a list of numbers with an even number of values?

   _____

   _____

Work It Out

Warm-Up 181

What's the Problem?   **Work It Out**

Hannah was bored during a long road trip to her grandparents' house for the holidays. She made a list of several of the posted speed limits she noticed on the trip.

Speed Limits (mph):

35	65	40
30	65	35
40	65	25
55	55	35
40	45	

1. **What is the mode of the speed limits?**

   _____

2. **What is the median speed limit?**

   _____

3. **What is the mean speed limit?**

   _____

· ·

Warm-Up 182

What's the Problem?   **Work It Out**

It took Hannah's dad 3 hours to drive the 120 miles to her grandparents' home.

What speed limit represents her dad's average speed during the trip?

_____

Warm-Up 183

What's the Problem?

Work It Out

Abigail's class took a very hard math test. The scores for the whole class are listed below. Abigail wanted to determine if her score was in the top quartile (top fourth of the class with the best scores) or in one of the lower quartiles.

Math Scores: 44, 100, 88, 65, 68, 68, 44, 96, 89, 68, 72, 76, 100, 92, 96, 64, 36, 40, 80, 84, 88, 92, 60, 66, 40, 56, 72, 100, 88, 80, 84, 96

- **Organize the 32 scores in order from highest to lowest in the box.**

- **Divide the scores in half with 16 upper and 16 lower scores.**

- **Divide each half in half again so that there are 4 quartiles.**

- -

Warm-Up 184

What's the Problem?

Work It Out

Abigail's math score was 80 and her friend, Amanda, received an 76.

1. **Which quartile was Abigail's score in?**

   _____

2. **Which quartile was Amanda's score in?**

   _____

Warm-Up 185

What's the Problem?

Helen and Sandy took a survey to determine how many hours the boys in their class played video games during the week of spring break. They recorded the hours on a chart.

1. **Organize the hours in order from least to greatest.**

   _____

   _____

2. **Compute the range of the numbers.** _____

3. **Determine the mode of the numbers. (There are 2 modes, so it's bimodal.)** _____

4. **Determine the median hours spent playing video games.** _____

5. **Determine the mean number of hours spent playing video games.** _____

Work It Out

Hours spent playing video games:

12	9	14
6	7	2
3	16	5
12	10	17
13	32	4
10	0	8

- -

Warm-Up 186

What's the Problem?

1. **Which number in the chart below is the outlier, the number far away from the range of the other numbers?**

12	9	14
6	7	2
3	16	5
12	10	17
13	32	4
10	0	8

   _____

2. **Which of the following numbers are the 2 outliers in this data list?**

   (1, 16, 27, 19, 20, 20, 21, 23, 58)

   _____

Work It Out

Data Analysis and Probability: line graphs

Warm-Up
187

What's the Problem?

Work It Out

As a part of his science project, Aiden recorded the temperature at the school playground in the sun at exactly noon for 10 days. He recorded the temperatures in degrees Fahrenheit.

Mon.	Tues.	Wed.	Thurs.	Fri.
73	74	72	76	79
Mon.	Tues.	Wed.	Thurs.	Fri.
71	73	72	72	70

1. **Graph the above data in a line graph.**

2. **What was the general pattern of temperatures over these 2 weeks?**

   _____

3. **Between which 2 consecutive days did the greatest change of temperature occur?**

   _____

Warm-Up
188

What's the Problem?

Work It Out

Study the line graph that Aiden made in the third week of measuring temperatures at noon.

1. **What was the general trend of noonday temperatures during the week?**

   _____

   _____

2. **What was the change of temperatures between Monday and Friday at noon?**

   _____

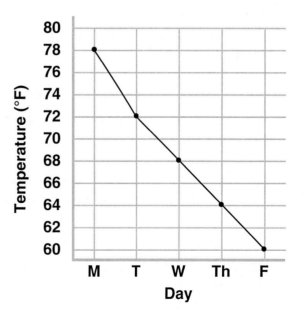

Warm-Up 189

What's the Problem?

Greg made a bar graph to illustrate the weights (in pounds) of some wild North American mammals.

1. **Which mammal on the graph weighs the least?**

   _____

2. **Which mammal on the graph weighs the most?**

   _____

3. **What is the range of weights on the graph?**

   _____

4. **Which 2 animals both weigh 18 pounds?**

   _____

5. **Which animal weighs twice as much as the red fox?**

   _____

Work It Out

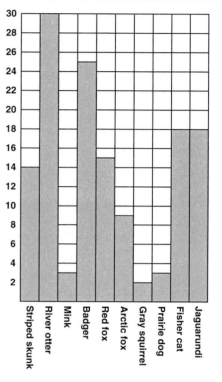

Warm-Up 190

What's the Problem?

Greg made this bar graph of lizard lengths (in inches).

1. **Which lizard is $\frac{1}{3}$ the length of the Gila monster?**

   _____

2. **Which 2 lizards together are as long as the collared lizard?**

   _____

3. **Which 3 lizards average 16 inches long?**

   _____

4. **Which lizard is 4 times as long as a banded gecko and 3 times as long as a green anole?**

   _____

Work It Out

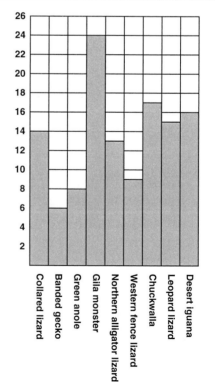

Warm-Up 191

What's the Problem?

Briana and Caroline made a double bar graph to compare how they spent their free time on the weekend.

1. How much more time did Briana spend reading than Caroline? _____

2. How much time did Caroline spend reading, playing an instrument, and in sports altogether? _____

3. Which girl spent more time doing chores? _____

4. How much total time did each girl account for?

   _____

5. Which activities each took 3 hours of Briana's weekend?

   _____

Work It Out

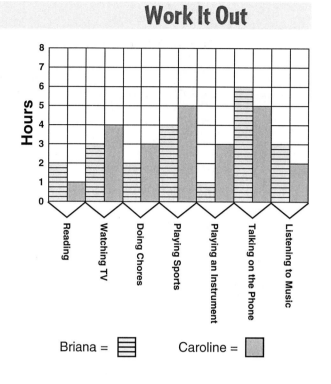

Warm-Up 192

What's the Problem?

Use the double bar graph about what Briana and Caroline did on the weekend to answer the following questions.

1. How much time did Caroline spend on music-related activities?

   _____

2. Who spent the most time on 1 activity? How much time did she spend?

   _____

3. Briana and Caroline both had very messy rooms. Who spent more time cleaning?

   _____

4. Which girl is probably more interested in sports? What does the graph indicate to support your opinion?

   _____

Work It Out

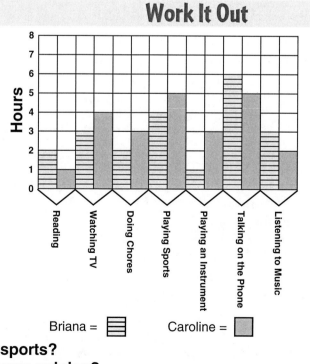

Warm-Up 193

What's the Problem?

Joseph and Joshua surveyed 65 boys about their favorite kinds of TV shows. Each boy chose his 2 favorite types of show. Joseph and Joshua recorded their information on the pictograph.

1. **Which kind of show got 50 votes?**

   _____

2. **How many more votes did comedy get than history?**

   _____

3. **Which 2 categories together equaled the votes for sports?**

   _____

4. **How many votes did action movies and nature/science get altogether?**

   _____

Work It Out

Favorite TV Shows—Boys

Sports	▭ ▭ ▭ ▭ ▭
Music Videos	▭ ▭ ▭
Comedy	▭ ▭
News	▭
Nature/Science	▭
History	▭
Action Movies	▭

Key: Each full ▭ represents 10 votes.

. . . .

Warm-Up 194

What's the Problem?

Ally and Amy surveyed 65 girls about their favorite kinds of TV shows. Each girl chose her 2 favorite types of show. Ally and Amy recorded their information on the pictograph.

1. **Which kind of show(s) got 35 votes?**

   _____

2. **Which kind of programming got the same number of votes from both the girls and the boys? 0**

   _____

3. **Which type of show interested the girls twice as much as the boys?**

   _____

4. **Which 2 types of shows were the least liked by the girls?**

   _____

Work It Out

Favorite TV Shows—Girls

Sports	▭ ▭
Music Videos	▭ ▭ ▭ ▭
Comedy	▭ ▭
News	▭
Nature/Science	▭
History	▭
Love Stories	▭ ▭ ▭ ▭

Key: Each full ▭ represents 10 votes.

Warm-Up 195

What's the Problem?

Jasmine planted 3 rows of corn seeds in her garden and kept a line graph of the fastest growing corn plant for 10 weeks.

1. How many inches had the corn grown by the second week? _____

2. How many inches did it grow from week 3 to week 6? _____

3. Between which weeks did it grow fastest? _____

4. During which weeks did it not get any taller? _____

5. What was the change in height over time of the corn plant during 10 weeks?

_____

Work It Out

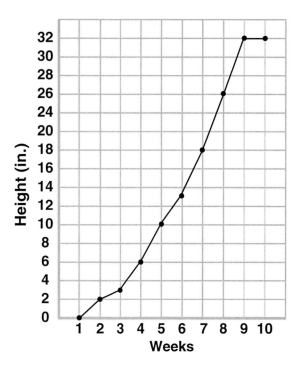

Warm-Up 196

What's the Problem?

Jasmine planted sunflowers and kept a line graph of the fastest growing sunflower over 10 weeks.

1. When did the sunflower grow 1 inch tall? _____

2. When did it reach 1 foot? _____

3. How many inches did it grow in 10 weeks? _____

4. How were the corn and sunflower plants alike and different in their changes over time?

_____

_____

_____

Work It Out

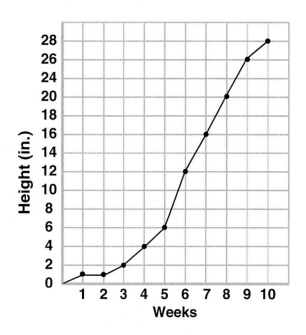

Warm-Up 197

What's the Problem?   **Work It Out**

Jason is playing a math game with 1 regular die with 6 sides. Rolling a 6 gives the player a huge advantage over his opponent. Rolling a 4 means he loses a turn, and rolling a 5 means he gets a chance to roll again. Rolling a 1 costs him only 1 point.

What is the probability that Jason . . .

1. will roll a 6? _____

2. will not roll a 2? _____

3. will have to lose a turn? _____

4. will roll an odd number? _____

5. will roll a factor of 6? _____

6. will roll a prime number? _____

- -

Warm-Up 198

What's the Problem?   **Work It Out**

In Jason's dice game, he wants to express his answers in terms of the odds of an event, written as the number of favorable outcomes compared to the number of unfavorable outcomes. Odds can be in favor of an event or against an event, and can be expressed as a fraction or as a ratio.

Odds (in favor of an event) = $\dfrac{\text{number of favorable outcomes}}{\text{number of unfavorable outcomes}}$

Odds (against an event) = $\dfrac{\text{number of unfavorable outcomes}}{\text{number of favorable outcomes}}$

Write the odds in favor of or against the following events from the dice game using the above formulas.

1. in favor of rolling a 5 = _____

2. against rolling a 3 = _____

3. in favor of rolling an even number = _____

4. against rolling a 7 = _____

5. in favor of rolling a factor of 2 = _____

Warm-Up 199

What's the Problem?

Freddy flipped a penny 10 times. He recorded the number of times the coin landed on heads and the number of times it landed on tails. He knew that he had 1 chance in 2 of flipping heads and the same chance of flipping tails. This is called *theoretical probability*.

Experimental probability is what actually happens. For example, Freddy flipped a coin 10 times and got 4 heads and 6 tails. In 20 flips, he had 9 heads and 11 tails.

1. **Flip a coin 16 times. Keep a record of the results in the chart.**

2. **What is the theoretical probability of the coin landing on heads out of 16 flips?**

   _____

3. **What was the experimental probability of your coin landing on heads?**

   _____

Work It Out

Flip	H or T?
1	
2	
3	
4	
5	
6	
7	
8	
9	
10	
11	
12	
13	
14	
15	
16	

Warm-Up 200

What's the Problem?

Freddy rolled 1 regular die with 6 sides—numbered 1, 2, 3, 4, 5, and 6—12 times. He recorded his results in the chart.

1. **What is the theoretical probability of rolling a 6?**

   _____

2. **What is Freddy's experimental probability of rolling a 6?**

   _____

3. **What is the theoretical probability of rolling a 5?**

   _____

4. **What is Freddy's experimental probability of rolling a 5?**

   _____

5. **What is the theoretical probability of rolling a 9?**

   _____

Work It Out

Roll	Result
1	4
2	5
3	2
4	1
5	5
6	6
7	6
8	1
9	3
10	4
11	5
12	5

Warm-Up 201

What's the Problem?

Work It Out

Marlene and Sabrina both bought tickets to a drawing for a huge bouquet of flowers at the fall carnival at their school. Marlene bought 10 tickets. Sabrina bought 15 tickets. There were 400 tickets sold for the drawing.

1. **What is the probability that Marlene will win the flowers?**

   _____

2. **What is the probability that Sabrina will win the flowers?**

   _____

3. **What is the probability that either Marlene or Sabrina will win the flowers?**

   _____

- -

Warm-Up 202

What's the Problem?

Work It Out

Lauren bought 25 tickets for the grand-prize drawing for monthly bouquets of flowers, and her friend Stephanie bought 20 tickets. 500 total tickets were sold for the drawing.

1. **What is the probability that Lauren will win the grand prize?**

   _____

2. **What is the probability that Stephanie will win the grand prize?**

   _____

3. **What is the probability that either Lauren or Stephanie will win the grand prize?**

   _____

Warm-Up 203

What's the Problem?   Work It Out

Dan took a survey of student preferences in the 6th grade. When he tabulated all of the results, he found that $\frac{5}{12}$ of the students like playing basketball, $\frac{5}{6}$ of the students like pizza, and $\frac{1}{2}$ of the students like playing video games.

1. **What is the probability that a student likes pizza and playing basketball?**

   _____

2. **What is the probability that a student likes pizza and playing video games?**

   _____

3. **What is the probability that a student likes to play basketball, play video games, and eat pizza?**

   _____

Warm-Up 204

What's the Problem?   Work It Out

Dan's survey of preferences found that $\frac{2}{3}$ of the 6th graders like jelly doughnuts, $\frac{1}{2}$ of them like sad movies, and $\frac{3}{4}$ of those surveyed like riding bikes.

1. **What is the probability that a student likes riding bikes and jelly doughnuts?**

   _____

2. **What is the probability that a student likes sad movies and jelly doughnuts?**

   _____

3. **What is the probability that a student likes jelly doughnuts, riding bikes, and sad movies?**

   _____

Warm-Up 205

What's the Problem?   **Work It Out**

Jennifer and Janice are twins whose names were in a class drawing for an opportunity to have lunch with the principal. There were 10 different names in the basket and 2 names would be drawn. The twins didn't care whose name was drawn first, but they both wanted to win.

What is the probability that both of their names would be drawn?

_____

Warm-Up 206

What's the Problem?   **Work It Out**

Jennifer and Janice had their names in a daily drawing at a shop in the mall that was giving away 2 of each new outfit. The shop's owners drew 2 names each day for 3 days. There were 20 different names in the drawing and the sisters wanted to win, but they did not care in which order their names were drawn.

What is the probability that both girls will have their names drawn on the first day?

_____

What's the Problem?

Work It Out

Christian is playing a card game with a regular deck of 52 cards. A player has an enormous advantage if he is dealt an ace.

1. **What is the probability that Christian will be dealt an ace from a full deck of cards?**

   _____

2. **What is the probability that he will be dealt either a king or an ace?**

   _____

3. **What is the probability that Christian will be dealt a face card (jack, queen, king)?**

   _____

- -

What's the Problem?

Work It Out

In a card game Christian is playing, the person having a red queen or a black jack has an advantage. In the game, 32 cards have been played, and neither a red queen nor a black jack have been dealt.

1. **What is the probability of being dealt a red queen or a black jack from a full deck of cards?**

   _____

2. **What is the probability of drawing a red queen or a black jack from the remaining cards in the game Christian is playing?**

   _____

What's the Problem?

Work It Out

Laura and Yvonne are playing a spelling game with wooden letter tiles. There are 8 tiles left with these letters:

The tiles are in a black bag and players can't see which tiles they are drawing. Laura gets to draw 2 tiles from the bag. She needs 2 *S*s to make a word.

What is the probability that Laura will draw 2 Ss back-to-back?

_____

• •

What's the Problem?

Work It Out

In the next round of the game, the following 6 letter tiles remained in the bag: S, T, R, E, I, N. Yvonne gets to draw 3 letter tiles. She needs to draw an E, an I, and an R to spell her word.

1. **What is the probability that Yvonne will draw a needed letter in her first pick?**

   _____

2. **What is the probability that Yvonne will draw all 3 of her needed letters in this round?**

   _____

Warm-Up 211

What's the Problem?

Work It Out

John needed to know the perimeter of a rectangular window box that his mother wanted him to get ready for planting. The length of the short side, he called *n*. The length of the long side, he called *x*. He discovered that the long side was twice the length of the shorter side.

1. **Write an equation for the perimeter using *n* and *x*.**

   _____

2. **Write a simplified equation using *n* because x = 2n.**

   _____

3. **Compute the perimeter for n = 6 inches.**

   _____

- -

Warm-Up 212

What's the Problem?

Work It Out

John needed to know the area of the window box to see if it would sit on the window in the kitchen.

1. **Write an equation to express the area in terms of *n* and *x*.**

   _____

2. **Write an equation to express the area in terms of *n*.**

   _____

3. **Compute the area for n = 6 inches.**

   _____

Algebra: working with variables; rate

Warm-Up 213

What's the Problem? Work It Out

Jared rode his bicycle 650 yards in 5 minutes. He wanted to determine his average speed in yards per minute. He used the formula: $r = \frac{d}{t}$, which means rate equals distance over time or rate equals distance divided by time.

1. **Write the equation for Jared's bicycle ride.**

   _____

2. **Solve the equation. How many yards per minute did he ride?**

   _____

Warm-Up 214

What's the Problem? Work It Out

Jared rode to his grandmother's house in 20 minutes. The distance he covered was 5,280 feet. He used the formula $r = \frac{d}{t}$ to compute his speed in feet per minute.

1. **Write the equation for Jared's ride to his grandmother's house.**

   _____

2. **Solve the equation. How many feet per minute did he ride?**

   _____

Warm-Up 215

What's the Problem?

Work It Out

Jasmine bought a present (p) for her mother that cost $42. The sales tax was 8%. She also had to pay $2 for gift wrapping. The gift-wrapping fee was not taxed. She wrote the algebraic expression below to show the total cost of the gift.

p + 0.08p + 2

(for p = 42 and 0.08p = 0.08 x 42)

Evaluate the expression. What was the total cost of the gift?

_____

Warm-Up 216

What's the Problem?

Work It Out

When Jasmine bought her grandmother a birthday gift (g), the price was $36. The sales tax was 8%. She had to pay $4 for gift wrapping. The gift-wrapping fee was not taxed.

1. **Write the algebraic expression for the total cost of the gift.**

   _____

2. **Evaluate the expression. What was the total cost of the gift?**

   _____

Warm-Up 217

What's the Problem?   **Work It Out**

Brittany was anxious to buy a new outfit for school. The total cost of the outfit was $87 including tax. Brittany had saved $61 toward the cost. She wrote the equation below to show how much more money she needed.

$$n + 61 = 87$$

Solve the equation. How much more money does she need?

_____

Warm-Up 218

What's the Problem?   **Work It Out**

Brittany wanted to purchase a pair of the newest style of jeans that cost $53 including tax. Her mother offered to pay $35 toward the cost, but Brittany has to save her allowances to pay for the remainder of the cost.

1. **Complete the equation to illustrate how much money Brittany has to save.**

   $$n + \underline{\hspace{2cm}} = \$53$$

2. **Solve the equation. How much more money does she need?**

   _____

What's the Problem?

Work It Out

Andrew grew tomatoes in his garden and sold them at a roadside stand in front of his house. The price he set for his tomatoes was 4 for a dollar. During a 1-hour period, he sold 48 tomatoes.

1. **Write an equation to show the sale and how much money (m) he made.**

   _____

2. **Solve the equation. How much money did Andrew receive?**

   _____

What's the Problem?

Work It Out

On one Saturday morning, Andrew earned $124 from his tomato sales. He sells 4 tomatoes for a dollar.

1. **Write an equation to show how many tomatoes (t) he sold that morning.**

   _____

2. **Solve the equation. How many tomatoes did he sell?**

   _____

What's the Problem?

Work It Out

Henry was uncertain which came first in doing order of operations. He knew the abbreviation was PEMDAS. He knew these were the 4 steps:

<u>Add and subtract</u> in order from left to right.

Do the work in the <u>parentheses</u>.

<u>Multiply and divide</u> in order from left to right.

Do the work with the <u>exponents</u>.

Place the steps in the correct order of operations.

_____

_____

_____

_____

- -

Warm–Up
222

What's the Problem?

Work It Out

Henry wrote this expression to illustrate the number of cards he had left in a card game.

$(9 \times 8 - 12) \div 6 - 4 + 5(5) - 20 + 4$

Evaluate the expression using the correct order of operations. How many cards did he have left?

_____

What's the Problem?

Work It Out

Amanda went shopping with her best friend. She spent $5 for a necklace and $3 for 1 pair of hoop earrings. She bought 3 plastic bracelets for $2 each and 4 rings for $2 each.

1. **Complete the expression to illustrate the cost of her purchases.**

   5 + 3 + (3 x _____) + (_____ x 2)

2. **Evaluate the expression. What was Brittany's total before sales tax?**

   _____

What's the Problem?

Work It Out

Amanda's best friend bought 7 rings at $2 each and 4 pairs of earrings at $6 each. She got a discount for multiple purchases, which divided the cost of these purchases by 2. She also bought a $4 necklace and a bracelet for $3.

1. **Complete the expression to illustrate the cost of her purchases.**

   [(7 x _____) + (4 x _____)] ÷ 2 + _____ + _____

2. **Evaluate the expression. What was Amanda's friend's total before sales tax?**

   _____

Warm-Up 225

What's the Problem?

Work It Out

Brian wrote the following expression to mathematically show the distance in inches around a model tower that he built.

$$5(a) - 4 + 3 \times 6 - 2(a)$$

(for $a = 5$)

Use the correct order of operations to evaluate his expression. How many inches is the distance around Brian's model tower?

_____

Warm-Up 226

What's the Problem?

Work It Out

Brian wrote this expression to mathematically show the distance in inches around a model castle that he constructed with small plastic blocks.

$$7 \times 8 + 6 - 4 + 3 \times 8 - 3(3)$$

Use the correct order of operations to evaluate his expression. How many inches is the distance around Brian's model castle?

_____

Warm-Up 227

What's the Problem?

Work It Out

Joseph told his twin brother, Samuel, "If you can solve this equation correctly, you will know exactly how many dollars I have hidden in my room."

$$(9 \times 8 \div 12 + 3 \times 4 \div 12) \div 7 = d$$

Solve the equation using the correct order of operations. How much money does Joseph have hidden in his room?

_____

Warm-Up 228

What's the Problem?

Work It Out

Samuel told his twin brother, Joseph, "If you can solve this equation correctly, you will know exactly how much money I have borrowed from your secret hiding place in the back of your closet."

$$(8 \times 12) \div 4 \times 3 + (4 + 24 + 8) \div 6 \times 8$$

Solve the equation using the correct order of operations. How much money did Samuel borrow?

_____

Warm-Up 229

What's the Problem? | Work It Out

Debbie asked Brianna, "Can you solve this problem in your head in less than 5 seconds? What is the sum of the products of 201 x 0, 2,111,332 x 0, and 1,234 x 0?"

1. Solve Debbie's math problem.

_____

2. Why were you able to solve it so quickly?

_____

_____

_____

Warm-Up 230

What's the Problem? | Work It Out

Brianna posed this problem to Debbie, "Can you solve these problems in less than 5 seconds? What number added to 6,578 equals 6,578 and what number times 6,578 equals 6,578?"

1. Solve Brianna's math problems. What are the answers?

_____

_____

2. Why were you able to solve them so quickly?

_____

_____

_____

Warm-Up 231

What's the Problem?   **Work It Out**

Anthony posed these math problems to his friend, Benny:

What number multiplied by $\frac{1}{4}$ equals 1?

What number multiplied by $\frac{2}{5}$ equals 1?

What number multiplied by $1 \frac{1}{4}$ equals 1?

1. Solve each problem.

_____

_____

_____

2. How can you do the problems in your mind?

_____

_____

_____

Warm-Up 232

What's the Problem?   **Work It Out**

Benny posed these math problems to Anthony:

What is the product of $-\frac{9}{5}$ and $-\frac{5}{9}$?

What number is the product of $\frac{2}{7}$ and $3 \frac{1}{2}$?

What is the product of $\frac{3}{13}$ and $\frac{13}{3}$?

1. Solve each problem.

_____

_____

_____

2. How can you do the problems in your mind?

_____

_____

_____

Algebra: functions

What's the Problem? Work It Out

Ashley made this table to show the relationship between numbers in a function.

1. **What is the function rule for the table?**

   _____

2. **Complete the table.**

3. **What is y when the value of x is 10?**

   _____

4. **What is y when the value of x is 13?**

   _____

Value of *x*	Function Rule x(___) + (___)	Value of *y*
3		13
4		16
5		_____
6		22
7		_____

• •

What's the Problem? Work It Out

Ashley made this table to show the relationship between numbers in a function.

1. **What is the function rule for the table?**

   _____

2. **Complete the table.**

Value of *x*	Function Rule 3(___) − (___)	Value of *y*
1		0
2		3
3		_____
4		_____
5		_____
6		15

Warm-Up 235

What's the Problem?

Anthony created this function table. He gave his friend Christopher a hint and 5 minutes to find the function rule.

Function rule hint: $(\underline{\hspace{1cm}} x)^2 - \underline{\hspace{1cm}}$

1. **What is the function rule?**

   _____

2. **Complete the table.**

Work It Out

Value of *x*	Function Rule $(\underline{\ } x)^2 - \underline{\ }$	Value of *y*
1		-3
2		9
3		29
4		_____
5		_____
6		_____
7		189

- -

Warm-Up 236

What's the Problem?

Christopher created this function table. He gave his friend Anthony a hint and 5 minutes to solve it.

Function rule hint: x^3

1. **What is the function rule?**

   _____

2. **Complete the table.**

Work It Out

Value of *x*	Function Rule x^3	Value of *y*
1		-2
2		5
3		24
4		_____
5		_____
6		_____
7		_____

Warm-Up 237

What's the Problem?   **Work It Out**

Kelly collected coins for game tickets at the school fair for 1 hour in the morning. She recorded her coins this way:

$$7n + 12d + 9n + 4q + 12n + 7q = 535$$

1. **Combine like terms to simplify the equation.**

   _____

2. **Determine the amount of money collected in nickels, dimes, and quarters for n = 5¢, d = 10¢, and q = 25¢.**

   _____

   _____

   _____

   _____

Warm-Up 238

What's the Problem?   **Work It Out**

In the afternoon, Kelly counted the following coins and recorded them this way:

$$3q + 5n + 5d + 18d + 7n + 4q + 3d + 2n = x$$

1. **Combine terms to simplify the equation.**

   _____

2. **Determine the amount of money (x) collected in nickels, dimes, and quarters for n = 5¢, d = 10¢, and q = 25¢.**

   _____

   _____

   _____

   _____

Warm-Up 239

What's the Problem?

Work It Out

Lauren's mother is 4 times as old as Lauren plus 3 years. Her mother is 43.

If *x* equals Lauren's age and 4x + 3 equals her mother's age of 43, the equation below can be used to find Lauren's age.

$$4x + 3 = 43$$

Solve the equation. How old is Lauren?

_____

Warm-Up 240

What's the Problem?

Work It Out

Lauren's mother is 6 times as old as her sister, Karen, plus 1 year. Her mother is 43.

1. **Write an equation where *x* equals Karen's age and 6x + 1 equals her mother's age of 43.**

   _____

2. **Solve the equation. How old is Karen?**

   _____

What's the Problem?

Work It Out

Susan's grandfather is 7 times older than she is plus 3 years. He is 66 years old.

1. **Write an equation where x equals Susan's age and 7x + 3 equals her grandfather's age of 66.**

   _____

2. **Solve the equation. How old is Susan?**

   _____

What's the Problem?

Work It Out

Susan's grandmother is 11 times older than Susan's sister, Lisa, plus 2 years. Her grandmother is 68 years old.

1. **Write an equation to express her grandmother's age.**

   _____

2. **Solve the equation. How old is Lisa?**

   _____

What's the Problem?

Kaitlyn is the marble champion of Meadowbrook School. She is especially fond of cat's eye marbles. She saves her babysitting money to purchase them from The Specialty Shoppe. Each cat's eye marble costs $3.75.

The below equation shows how much the marbles cost.

c = 3.75m

1. **Complete the table to show how much it will cost to purchase these marbles.**

2. **How much would Kaitlyn spend on 12 cat's eye marbles?**

_____

Work It Out

Marbles (m)	Cost (c)
1	$3.75
2	$7.50
3	
4	
5	
6	

What's the Problem?

Kaitlyn buys regular marbles for $1.75 a bag. Each bag has 100 marbles.

1. **Write an equation to show how much the marble bags cost.**

_____

2. **Complete the table to show how much it will cost to purchase these bags of marbles.**

3. **How much would Kaitlyn spend on 14 bags of marbles?**

_____

Work It Out

Marble Bags (b)	Cost (c)
1	$1.75
2	
3	
4	
5	
6	

Warm-Up 245

What's the Problem?

Albert graphed a linear equation to show how much weight he is losing during his spring training workout for football. In the equation, *y* equals the ounces he is losing and *x* is the hours he is spending exercising during the week.

The equation is $y = 2(x) + 3$.

1. **Substitute the numbers 1, 2, 3, 4, 5, and 6 for *x* in the equation and graph the results. The first 2 are graphed for you.**

2. **Does the equation produce a straight line on the graph?**

_____

Work It Out

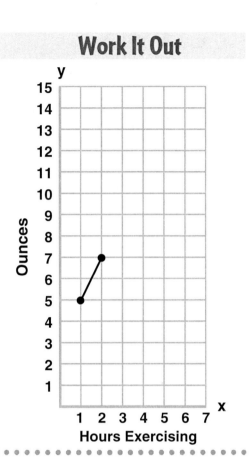

Ounces

Hours Exercising

Warm-Up 246

What's the Problem?

Albert produced the equation $y = x + 1$ for the graph to the right to show the number of cups of water he was drinking during and after exercise over the course of a week.

Substitute the numbers 1, 2, 3, 4, 5, 6, 7, 8, 9, and 10 for *x* in the equation and graph the results. The first 3 are graphed for you.

Work It Out

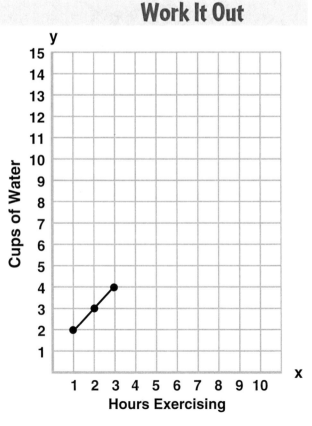

Cups of Water

Hours Exercising

Algebra: distributive property of multiplication

What's the Problem?   **Work It Out**

Russell wrote this expression to illustrate the number of jelly doughnuts sold at his favorite bakery on 3 separate mornings:

d(15) + d(22) + d(18)

Each doughnut (d) cost $1.25.

Evaluate the expression to determine the total amount spent on jelly doughnuts by patrons of the bakery.

_____

What's the Problem?   **Work It Out**

Russell wrote this expression to illustrate the number of chocolate éclairs purchased by patrons at his favorite bakery on 3 separate mornings: c(12) + c(9) + c(19). Each chocolate éclair cost $1.95.

Evaluate the expression to determine the total amount spent on chocolate éclairs by patrons of the bakery.

_____

Warm-Up 249

What's the Problem?

Work It Out

Christian liked to pose questions to Andrew, his best friend and strongest competitor in math. He asked him to find the fractional number exactly equal in distance on a number line between each of these pairs of fractions:

Pair 1: $\frac{2}{4}$ and $\frac{3}{4}$

Pair 2: $\frac{5}{8}$ and $\frac{6}{8}$

Pair 3: $\frac{5}{6}$ and $\frac{6}{6}$

Which fractional number is exactly equal in distance on a number line between each pair of fractions? Draw number lines to help you.

_____

_____

_____

Warm-Up 250

What's the Problem?

Work It Out

Andrew posed this question in turn for his friend, Christian. He asked him to find the one decimal number exactly equal in distance on a number line between each of these pairs of decimals:

Pair 1: 9.1 and 9.2

Pair 2: 0.43 and 0.44

Pair 3: 2.12 and 2.13

Which decimal number is exactly equal in distance on a number line between each pair of decimals?

_____

_____

_____

ANSWER KEY

Warm-Up 1

Lauren should find 24 numbers.

9751	7951	5917	1597
9715	7915	5971	1579
9517	7591	5179	1795
9571	7519	5197	1759
9157	7195	5719	1957
9175	7159	5791	1975

Warm-Up 2

295 is the given number. Rearrange these digits to find other numbers:

259   529   592   925   952

The digits 3, 5, and 6 also equal 90 when multiplied together. Rearrange these digits to find other numbers:

356	536	635
365	563	653

Warm-Up 3

There are 13 combinations using at least 1 quarter, 1 dime, and 1 nickel.

3Q, 2D, 1N	1Q, 7D, 1N
3Q, 1D, 3N	1Q, 6D, 3N
	1Q, 5D, 5N
2Q, 4D, 2N	1Q, 4D, 7N
2Q, 3D, 4N	1Q, 3D, 9N
2Q, 2D, 6N	1Q, 2D, 11N
2Q, 1D, 8N	1Q, 1D, 13N

Warm-Up 4

There are 29 total palindromes between 0 and 300.

Palindromes between 0 and 100:
  11, 22, 33, 44, 55, 66, 77, 88, 99

Palindromes between 101 and 200:
  101, 111, 121, 131, 141, 151, 161, 171, 181, 191

Palindromes between 201 and 300:
  202, 212, 222, 232, 242, 252, 262, 272, 282, 292

Warm-Up 5

Jimmy

Monday	Tuesday	Wednesday	Thursday	Friday
swimming	swimming	swimming	swimming	swimming
basketball	volleyball	basketball	volleyball	basketball
reading	reading	reading	reading	reading
tennis	running	tennis	running	tennis

Allison

Monday	Tuesday	Wednesday	Thursday	Friday
swimming	swimming	swimming	swimming	swimming
reading	reading	reading	reading	reading
gymnastics	table tennis	gymnastics	table tennis	gymnastics
running	softball	running	softball	running

Warm-Up 6

There are 20 possible combinations.

D—C	C—D	M—D	A—D	B—D
D—M	C—M	M—C	A—C	B—C
D—A	C—A	M—A	A—M	B—M
D—B	C—B	M—B	A—B	B—A

Warm-Up 7

1,048,576 pennies = $10,485.76

Bag	Pennies		Bag	Pennies
1	1		11	1,024
2	2		12	2,048
3	4		13	4,096
4	8		14	8,192
5	16		15	16,384
6	32		16	32,768
7	64		17	65,536
8	128		18	131,072
9	256		19	262,144
10	512		20	524,288
			21	1,048,576

Warm-Up 8

45, 90, 135, and 180 can be divided evenly by 3, 5, and 9. Start by making a list of the multiples of 5 between 5 and 200. This automatically eliminates those numbers between 1 and 200 that are not evenly divisible by 5.

Then find the sum of the digits in each of the numbers. If the sum is evenly divisible by 3, then the number is evenly divisible by 3. For example, in the number 45, 4 + 5 = 9, which is evenly divisible by 3; so 45 is divisible by 3. In the number 65, 6 + 5 = 11, which is not evenly divisible by 3; so 65 is not divisible by 3. Cross out all of the numbers in your list that are not divisible by 3.

Now look at the remaining numbers and do the same for the number 9 as you did for 3. Find the sum of each of the digits in the remaining numbers. If the sum is evenly divisible by 9, then the number is evenly divisible by 9. Cross out all of the numbers in your list that are not divisible by 9. This should leave 45, 90, 135, and 180.

Warm-Up 9

She placed 22 quarters in the 8th pile. She used 92 total quarters in all 8 piles.

Pile	Quarters
1	1
2	4
3	7
4	10
5	13
6	16
7	19
8	22

Warm-Up 10

There are 8 possible combinations.

Ace, 2

King, 3

Queen, 3

Jack, 3

10, 3

9, 4

8, 5

7, 6

Warm-Up 11

They will make 28 total handshakes.

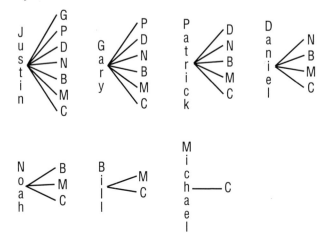

Warm-Up 12

There are 45 total gift exchanges.

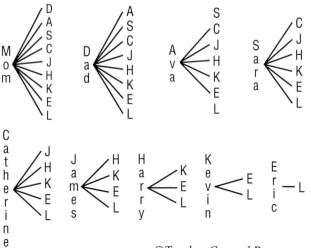

Warm-Up 13

It took 5 rounds to get a winner.

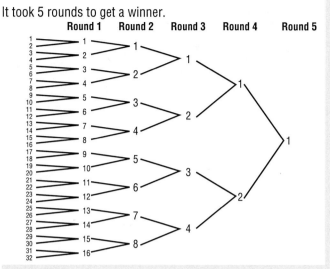

Warm-Up 14

There are 40 possible outfit combinations.

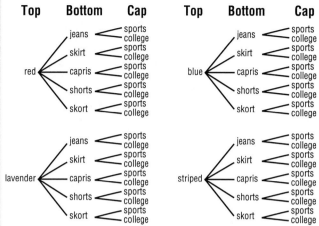

Warm-Up 15

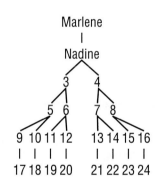

Warm-Up 16

Prime factors of 72: 2 x 2 x 2 x 3 x 3

Prime factors of 96: 2 x 2 x 2 x 2 x 2 x 3

96 has more prime factors.

Possible tree diagrams:

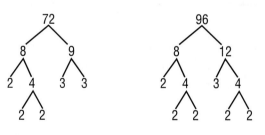

Warm-Up 17

Prime factors of 999: 3 x 3 x 3 x 37

Prime factors of 144: 2 x 2 x 2 x 2 x 3 x 3

Raphael's number (144) has more prime factors.

Possible tree diagrams:

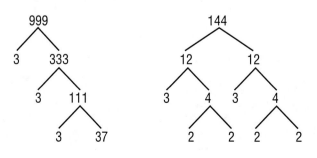

Warm-Up 18

31 people knew the secret after the 4th set of friends were told.

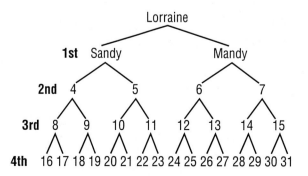

Warm-Up 19

Kevin used 40 pennies in his diagram.

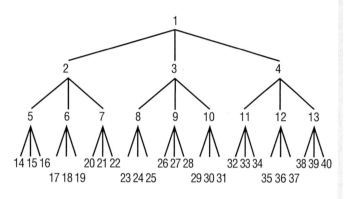

Warm-Up 20

There are 24 possible combinations.

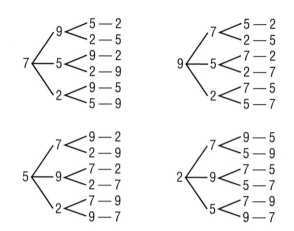

Warm-Up 21

Alicia = 14 + Irene
Mary = Irene – 6
Mary = 9 + Kathy
Alicia + Sarah = 71
Jolene = Sarah – 7
Maybeth = 2 x Mary
Sarah = 41

Sarah = 41 books
Jolene = 41 – 7 = 34 books
Alicia + 41 = 71; Alicia = 30 books
30 = 14 + Irene; Irene = 16 books
Mary = 16 – 6 = 10 books
10 = 9 + Kathy; Kathy = 1 book
Maybeth = 2 x 10 = 20 books

Warm-Up 22

Carlos started with $14,000.

$3,000 left

+ $3,000 (lost in land deal)

+ $4,000 (paid taxes)

– $1,000 (earned rent)

+ $5,000 (bought property)

$14,000 to start with

Warm-Up 23

Kevin's number is 540.
The number:

must have 3 digits (between 500 and 800).

must end in 0 because it is divisible by 10.

must be divisible by 9, so the total of the digits added together must equal 9.

Choices are 540, 630, 720.
The number:

cannot have a 2, so 720 is not the number.

must be divisible by 4, so 630 is not the number.

So the answer is 540.

Warm-Up 24

Jeremiah = 2 + Jeffrey
Jeremiah = Justin – 3
James = Jeffrey – 2
James = 3 + Jack
Jack = 2 + Jonathan
Jonathan = 1
Jordan = Jeremiah

Jonathan = 1 year old
Jack = 2 + 1 = 3 years old
James = 3 + 3 = 6 years old
6 = Jeffrey – 2; Jeffrey = 8 years old
Jeremiah = 2 + 8 = 10 years old
Jordan = 10 years old
10 = Justin – 3; Justin = 13 years old

Warm-Up 25

Pile	1st	2nd	3rd	4th	5th	6th	7th	8th	9th	10th
Pennies	1	1	2	3	5	8	13	21	34	55

Pattern = add 2 consecutive piles to get the next pile
(Fibonacci sequence)

Warm-Up 26

8 candy bars to Cindy
8 candy bars to Jackie
16 candy bars to Samantha
+ 32 candy bars to Ashley
——————————————
64 candy bars in the bag

Warm-Up 27

Age	Charms
11	3
10	6
9	6
8	6
7	6
6	6

Total 33 charms beginning on her birthday at age 6.

She will receive 1 charm at Easter, the next celebration.

Warm-Up 28

7 players in the game.
The last player got 1 point.

Player	Points
1	64
2	32
3	16
4	8
5	4
6	2
7	1

Warm-Up 29

James had $400 to start with.

$75 left
$25 parent gift
$100 helmet/racing outfit
+ $200 dirt bike
——————————
$400 to start

Warm-Up 30

Player	Cards
Hannah	2
Sarah	4
Briana	8
Yvonne	16
Jennifer	32
Kristin	64

Warm-Up 31

There are 50 sets of numbers equaling 101.

100 + 1 = 101
99 + 2 = 101
98 + 3 = 101
97 + 4 = 101
etc.

101 x 50 = 5,050

Warm-Up 32

April's total was $230.95 before tax.
Round each price to the nearest dollar and add:

18 + 23 + 60 + 10 + 120 = 231

Subtract 1 cent from each item from the above total:

$231.00 − $0.05 = $230.95

Warm-Up 33

Round each amount to the nearest quarter and add:
.25 + .50 + .75 + .50 + .25 + .50 + .75 + 1.00 + .50 + 1.00
+ .25 + .50 + 1.00 = $7.75

Add pairs of numbers that make simpler numbers then add total:

.23 + .77 = 1.00
.27 + .73 = 1.00
.54 + .47 = 1.01
.99 + .21 = 1.20
1.02 + .48 = 1.50
1.06 + .49 = 1.55
Actual Total = 7.26 + .50 = $7.76

Warm-Up 34

Nicole needs 22 toothpicks to make the fence.
She uses 4 toothpicks for the first section, but for each section thereafter she only adds 3 more toothpicks. This creates a pattern, 4 for the first section plus 3 times the number of sections equals the number of toothpicks:

Section	Toothpicks
1	4
2	4 + 3 = 7
3	4 + (3 x 2) = 10
4	4 + (3 x 3) = 13
5	4 + (3 x 4) = 16
6	4 + (3 x 5) = 19
7	4 + (3 x 6) = 22

Warm-Up 35

Notice that every 2 numbers added together make a simpler number. Add each set of 2 numbers to make simpler numbers, and then add to find the total.

$11
$19 → $30

$27
$13 → $40

$8
$22 → $30

$79
$21 → $100

Total = $200

Warm-Up 36

Possible method 1:
Round each amount to the nearest quarter and add:
1.50 + .75 + .50 + .25 + .25 + .25 + .75 + .50 + 1.75 = 6.50
Estimated total = $6.50

Possible method 2:
Estimate the totals using multiples of quarters:

$1.50 (6)
$0.75 (3)
$0.55 (2)
$0.22 (1)
$0.28 (1)
$0.20 (1)
$0.75 (3)
$0.50 (2)
$1.75 (7)

Total = 26 quarters
26 x $0.25 = $6.50

Warm-Up 37

Cousin	Greetings
Jill	11 (1 to each cousin)
Mary	10 (already greeted Jill)
Larry	9 (already greeted Jill and Mary)
Sarah	8 (already greeted 3 cousins)
Maria	7 (already greeted 4 cousins)
Joey	6 (already greeted 5 cousins)
Kenny	5 (already greeted 6 cousins)
Cindy	4 (already greeted 7 cousins)
Sammy	3 (already greeted 8 cousins)
Jane	2 (already greeted 9 cousins)
Regis	1 (already greeted 10 cousins)
Tony	0 (already greeted everyone)

Total Greetings = 66

Warm-Up 38

Jonah will add 51 numbers.

Add the first even number and the last even number in the set. Then add the second even number and the second-to-last even number in the set. Continue until you reach the middle of the set:

900 + 1,000 = 1,900
902 + 998 = 1,900
904 + 996 = 1,900
906 + 994 = 1,900
etc.
948 + 952 = 1,900
950

There are 25 sets of even numbers equaling 1,900.

Multiply 25 times 1,900, which equals 47,500. Add the 950 in the middle of the set, making a total of 48,450.

Warm-Up 39

David's report was 54 pages long.

Pages	Digits
1–9	9
10–19	20
20–29	20
30–39	20
40–49	20
50–54	+ 10
	99 (total)

Warm-Up 40

The organism weighed 512 grams after 30 minutes.

Grams	Minutes
1	3
2	6
4	9
8	12
16	15
32	18
64	21
128	24
256	27
512	30

Warm-Up 41

Choices: 64, 17, 6, and 4

Edgar (4) = cubic root of Elijah (64)
Eugene = 1 x 2 x 3 = (6)
Ernest = prime number = (17)

Warm-Up 42

Madison = 66
Mariah = 45
Jewel = 36
Cheryl = 13
Alexis = 1

Warm-Up 43

Sandy and Hazel each scored 83%.

If the average score for the 4 tests was 87 (given), the total for all tests must be 4 times 87 because to find the average you divide the total by 4 to get 87.

    4 x 87 = 348

Two test scores are given, 100 and 82.

    100 + 82 = 182

Subtract 182 from the total to get the total of the 2 unknown scores.

    348 – 182 = 166

Divide 166 by 2 to get each girl's score.

    166 ÷ 2 = 83

Warm-Up 44

Starting number on odometer = 23,932

The next number on the odometer that would be a palindrome is 24,   042.

Warm-Up 45

2 cm x 1 cm x 4 cm = 8 cu. cm (per block)

8 cm x 160 cm = 1,280 cu. cm (for all the blocks)

Possible answers:

8 cm x 8 cm x 20 cm holds all blocks exactly

10 cm x 8 cm x 16 cm holds all blocks exactly

Warm-Up 46

The answer to Peter's puzzle is 9.

The answer to Peter's puzzle must be the largest single-digit number that divides evenly into the 4 number options listed.

Single-digit number choices = 1 through 9

Use divisibility rules starting with the largest number, 9, and work your way down to see which numbers divide evenly.

Divisibility rule for 9: Find the sum of all the digits in a number. If the sum is divisible by 9, so is the number.

This works for all 4 numbers, so the answer is 9.

Warm-Up 47

Jerry is currently reading pages 91 and 92.

If Jerry is about a quarter through the book, divide the total pages by 4 to get an estimated starting point.

    389 ÷ 4 = 97.25

Start with pages 97 and 98, and go higher or lower depending on the answer. The product of Jerry's page numbers is 8,372.

    97 x 98 = 9,506 (too high)

    95 x 96 = 9,120 (too high)

    93 x 94 = 8,742 (too high)

    92 x 93 = 8,556 (too high)

    91 x 92 = 8,372 (correct answer)

Warm-Up 48

Jackie's farm has 14 cows and 27 chickens.

If there are 41 total animals, start with a nearly even number cows and chickens. Work down and up until you get a total of 110 legs and 41 animals.

Cows (4 legs)	Chickens (2 legs)	Total
20 (80 legs)	21 (42 legs)	122 legs
16 (64 legs)	25 (50 legs)	114 legs
15 (60 legs)	26 (52 legs)	112 legs
14 (56 legs)	27 (54 legs)	110 legs

Warm-Up 49

Drinks	Side Orders	Toppings
cola (James)	regular fries (Cherrie)	ketchup (James)
lemonade (Jasmine)	curly fries (James)	barbeque sauce (Jasmine)
juice (Cherrie)	cheese fries (Jasmine)	lettuce (Anna)
milk (Anna)	chips (Anna)	tomatoes (Cherrie)

Warm-Up 50

Alicia = 2 + Amy

Alicia = 10 + Alexis

Allison = 5

Allison = 2 + Alexis

Mother = Alicia + Amy + Allison + Alexis

Allison = 5 years old

Allison (5) = 2 + Alexis; Alexis = 3 years old

Alicia = 10 + 3 = 13 years old

Alicia (13) = 2 + Amy; Amy = 11 years old

Mother = 13 + 11 + 5 + 3 = 32 years old

ANSWER KEY *(cont.)*

Warm-Up 51
1. 12
2. 4/5
3. GCF = 2; 19/24

Warm-Up 52
Fractions A, B, D, E, F, and G can be reduced using Jasmine's system.

Warm-Up 53
1. Kari
2. 9/16 total
3. 7/16 left

Warm-Up 54
1. Kari
2. the whole cake (15/15)
3. no cake was left

Warm-Up 55
$1.90

Warm-Up 56
$3.05

Warm-Up 57
1. 57
2. 24%

Warm-Up 58
1. 32
2. 8
3. 20%

Warm-Up 59
1. 47
2. 13
3. 21.7% or 22%

Warm-Up 60
1. Ruth = 6; Jess = 10; Yvonne = 16
2. 18
3. 36%

Warm-Up 61
1. $15.20
2. $60.80

Warm-Up 62
1. $8.22
2. $24.66

Warm-Up 63
$333 \div 9 = 37$
$126{,}063 \div 9 = 14{,}007$
$277{,}227 \div 9 = 30{,}803$
$111{,}222{,}333 \div 9 = 12{,}358{,}037$
$345{,}678{,}678 \div 9 = 38{,}408{,}742$

Warm-Up 64
3 has the same divisibility rule as 9.

Warm-Up 65
1. 4/90 = 2/45 cup
2. 46/90 = 23/45 cup

Warm-Up 66
1 cup total (18/18)

Warm-Up 67
A. 3.6×10^7
B. 6.7×10^7
C. 9.3×10^7
D. 1.41×10^8
E. 4.8×10^8
F. 8.87×10^8
G. 1.8×10^9
H. 2.8×10^9
I. 3.6×10^9

Warm-Up 68
A. 1.7×10^{24}
B. 1×10^{16}
C. 1.41×10^{18}
D. 4.8915×10^{24}
E. 1.5262×10^{14}

Warm-Up 69
1. -1
2. 7
3. -6

Warm-Up 70
1. Opposite values in order on number line: -13, -12, -9, -7, -6, -2, 0, 1, 3, 4, 11, 14
2. 14
3. -13
4. 1

Warm-Up 71
Prime: 2, 3, 5, 7, 11, 13, 17, 19, 23 (2 = only even prime)
Composite: 4, 6, 8, 9, 10, 12, 14, 15, 16, 18, 20, 21, 22, 24, 25
Neither: 1

Warm-Up 72
$3 \times 8 = 24$ (odd prime)
$1 \times 15 = 15$ (composite)
$10 \times 1 = 10$ (neither)
$10 \times 1 = 10$ (even prime)
Total points = 59

Warm-Up 73
1. 25: 1, 5, 25
   36: 1, 2, 3, 4, 6, 9, 12, 18, 36
   48: 1, 2, 3, 4, 6, 8, 12, 16, 24, 48
   64: 1, 2, 4, 8, 16, 32, 64
   96: 1, 2, 3, 4, 6, 8, 12, 16, 24, 32, 48, 96
   100: 1, 2, 4, 5, 10, 20, 25, 50, 100
2. 96 (12 factors)

Warm-Up 74
1. 80: 1, 2, 4, 5, 8, 10, 16, 20, 40, 80
   120: 1, 2, 3, 4, 5, 6, 8, 10, 12, 15, 20, 24, 30, 40, 60, 120
2. GCF = 40

Warm-Up 75
1. Start with 11^2 then 12^2, etc., until you reach a number close to, but under 200.
2. 196 (14^2)

Warm-Up 76
1. 484 (22^2)
2. yes
3. 961 (31^2)

Warm-Up 77
1. $100 cost
2. $50 saved

Warm-Up 78
1. $60 cost
2. $60 saved

Warm-Up 79
1. paid $61.21
2. saved $84.54

Warm-Up 80
1. paid $74.25
2. saved $35.75

Warm-Up 81
1. 12 hits
2. 22 at bats
3. .545

Warm-Up 82
1. .452
2. .440
3. .446
4. yes

Warm-Up 83
1. 60%
2. 62.5% or 63%
3. Charles

Warm-Up 84
1. 77.8% or 78%
2. 77.8% or 78%
3. same

Warm-Up 85
63.6%

Warm-Up 86
77.5%

Warm-Up 87
1. 57 hours
2. 47.5 hours
3. 9.5 hours

Warm-Up 88
1. 36.25 m.p.h.
2. 48.33 m.p.h.

Warm-Up 89
1. 62.5 gallons
2. $218.75

Warm-Up 90
1. 30 gallons
2. $102

Warm-Up 91
1. 800 sq. ft.
2. 80 ft.

Warm-Up 92
88.9 sq. yd. or 89 sq. yd.

Warm-Up 93
1. 10,800 sq. ft.   3. 800 sq. ft.
2. 4,800 sq. ft.   4. 5,200 sq. ft.

Warm-Up 94
1. 577.8 sq. yd. or 578 sq. yd.
2. 420 ft.

Warm-Up 95
1. 960 cu. in.
2. No, only 960 blocks will fit.

Warm-Up 96
The cube will be 10 in. long,
10 in. wide, and 10 in. high.

Warm-Up 97
Triangle: 3; 60°; 180°
Square: 4; 90°; 360°
Pentagon: 5; 108°; 540°
Hexagon: 6; 120°; 720°
Octagon: 8; 135°; 1,080°
Nonagon: 9; 140°; 1,260°
Decagon: 10; 144°; 1,440°
Dodecagon: 12; 150°; 1,800°

Warm-Up 98
1. dodecagon
2. dodecagon

Warm-Up 99
P of triangle ABC = 14 ft.
P of triangle ACD = 15.5 ft.

Warm-Up 100
A of triangle A = 8.75 sq. ft.
A of triangle B = 11.25 sq. ft.

Warm-Up 101
48 sq. in.

Warm-Up 102
Possible answer:

Warm-Up 103
Box D is the best fit.

Warm-Up 104
Box C

Warm-Up 105
1. C = 37.68 in.
2. A = 113.04 sq. in.

Warm-Up 106
1. C = 62.8 in.
2. A = 314 sq. in.

Warm-Up 107
1. C = 56.52 in.
2. A = 254.34 sq. in.

Warm-Up 108
V = 6,280 cu. in.

Warm-Up 109
864 sq. in.

Warm-Up 110
55 sq. ft.

Warm-Up 111
600 cu. ft.

Warm-Up 112
1. 4,200 sq. ft.   2. 466.7 sq. yd.

Warm-Up 113
Alex's home = (8, 10)
Grocery store = (10, 3)
Pizza parlor = (13, 5)
School = (3, 2)
Small farm = (15, 10)
Convenience store = (11, 1)

Warm-Up 114
(4, 7) Friends Park
(6, 1) Elm Park
(15, 10) Small farm
(3, 10) Mark's home
(10, 3) Grocery store
(3, 2) School
(13, 5) Pizza parlor

Warm-Up 115
(15, 1) Chewing gum
(2, 13) Super hero cards
(12, 7) DVD
(8, 3) Empty box
(5, 9) Cookies
(15, 15) Baseball
(11, 13) Yo-yo
(8, 5) Remote control
(10, 10) Candy bar

Warm-Up 116
Marbles (2, 6)
Cookies (5, 9)
DVD (12, 7)
Chewing gum (15, 1)
Candy bar (10, 10)
Chips (1, 2)
Baseball (15, 15)
Yo-yo (11, 13)

Warm-Up 117
(9, -3) Heidi, IV
(9, 7) Betty, I
(-6, -6) Elana, III
(-4, -3) Fern, III
(-4, 4) Cindy, II

(6, -6) Georgia, IV
(-6, 6) Delilah, II
(3, 4) Allison, I

Warm-Up 118
Charlene (0, 0)
Allison (3, 4)
Betty (9, 7)
Cindy (-4, 4)
Delilah (-6, 6)
Elana (-6, -6)
Fern (-4, -3)
Georgia (6, -6)
Heidi (9, -3)

Warm-Up 119
Jodelle's dolls (4, 4)
Coins (-8, 8)
Secret #1 (-9, -8)
Secret #2 (8, -8)
Candy cache (4, -4)
Paper money (8, 8)
Cards (-4, -4)
Marbles (-4, 4)

Warm-Up 120
Check graph for accuracy.

Warm-Up 121
∠1 = 60°   ∠5 = 60°
∠2 = 120°   ∠6 = 120°
∠3 = 120°   ∠7 = 120°
∠4 = 60°   ∠8 = 60°

Warm-Up 122
1. Angles 1, 4, 5, and 8 as equal.
   Angles 2, 3, 6, and 7 as equal.
2. ∠1 + ∠2 = 180°
3. Two angles that add up to 180°
   are supplementary, such as ∠1
   and 2, ∠3 and 4, ∠5 and 6, and
   ∠7 and 8.
4. Opposite angles include ∠1 and
   4, ∠2 and 3, ∠5 and 8, and ∠6
   and 7.

Warm-Up 123
1. 360 degrees
2. A = 80°
   B = 40°
   C = 60°
   D = 80°
   E = 40°
   F = 60°
3. little brothers = B and E
   parents = A and D
   Sabrina + sister = C and F

ANSWER KEY (cont.)

Warm-Up 124
1. 360°   3. 30°
2. 60°   4. 2

Warm-Up 125
Shape name: isosceles right triangle
∠A = 45°
∠B = 90°
∠C = 45°
Shapes: square, triangle, parallelogram

Warm-Up 126
Shape name: isosceles triangle
∠D = 30°
∠E = 120°
∠F = 30°
Shape: triangle

Warm-Up 127
1. 18 in.
2. 1,017.36 sq. in.
3. 24,416.64 cu. in.

Warm-Up 128
113.04 in.

Warm-Up 129
4 dominoes

Warm-Up 130
13 dominoes

Warm-Up 131
1. about 7 pennies
2. about 70 pennies
3. about 700 pennies

Warm-Up 132
1. about 17 pennies
2. about 204 pennies
3. about 612 pennies

Warm-Up 133
1. 9 in. long and 7 in. wide
2. A = 35 sq. in.
3. P = 24 in.
4. A = 63 sq. in.
5. P = 32 in.

Warm-Up 134
1. A = 320 sq. in.
2. A (brother) = 24 sq. in.
   A (3 friends) = 16 sq. in.
   A (mom) = 36 sq. in.
   A (dad) = 12 sq. in.
3. A = 232 sq. in.

Warm-Up 135
The triangles cannot be drawn. Two smaller sides of a triangle cannot be equal or less in length than the third side.

Warm-Up 136
These triangles can be drawn. The two smaller sides are greater than the length of the longer side.

Warm-Up 137
1. A = 300 sq. ft.
2. A = 112.5 sq. ft.
3. 412.5 sq. ft.
4. 21 boxes

Warm-Up 138
1. 92 feet
2. 460 seedlings

Warm-Up 139
1. Total A = 32 sq. ft.
2. A = 16 sq. ft.

Warm-Up 140
1. A = 360 sq. ft.
2. A = 180 sq. ft.
3. P = 20 + 18 + 27 = 65 ft.

Warm-Up 141
1. P = 880 ft.
2. A = 30,000 sq. ft.

Warm-Up 142
1. P = 1,480 ft.
2. A = 100,000 sq. ft.

Warm-Up 143
Answers will vary.

Warm-Up 144
Large cone—14 grams
Deer bone—112 grams
Antlers—196 grams
Scallop shell—21 grams
Abalone shell—56 grams
Shell guide—112 grams
Field guide—336 grams

Warm-Up 145
1. sea lion = 4 oz.
   dolphin = 6 oz.
   calf = 2 oz.
   sea otter = 1 1/3 oz.
2. sea lion = 112 grams
   dolphin = 168 grams
   calf = 56 grams
   sea otter = 37 1/3 grams

Warm-Up 146
1. hammerhead = 4 oz.
   megamouth = 5 1/3 oz.
   great white = 5 2/3 oz.
2. hammerhead = 112 grams
   megamouth = 149 1/3 grams
   great white = 158 2/3 grams

Warm-Up 147
1. acute
2. obtuse
3. acute
4. acute
5. acute
6. obtuse

Warm-Up 148
1. right angle, 90°
2. reflex angle, 270°
3. obtuse

Warm-Up 149
The blue box because its volume is 343 cu. cm. The volume of the other boxes is less than 300 cu. cm, which is the minimum size needed to hold all of the cubes.

Warm-Up 150
Answers will vary. Mariah needs a box that is 300 cu. cm. Possible answers:
10 cm x 10 cm x 3 cm
6 cm x 5 cm x 10 cm
3 cm x 5 cm x 20 cm

Warm-Up 151
1. 4,320 times per hour
2. 103,680 times per day
3. 4,560 times per hour
4. 109,440 times per day

Warm-Up 152
1. 4,800 times per hour
2. 115,200 times per day
3. 5,040 times per hour
4. 120,960 times per day

Warm-Up 153
175 days

Warm-Up 154
289 days

Warm-Up 155
1. 27 degrees cooler
2. 39 degrees cooler
3. 57 degrees cooler

Warm-Up 156
1. 27 degrees colder
2. 45 degrees colder
3. 54 degrees colder

Warm-Up 157
1. Celsius
2. Fahrenheit

Warm-Up 158
1. 588 degrees hotter
2. 768 degrees hotter
3. 664 degrees hotter

Warm-Up 159
C = 6.28 inches

Warm-Up 160
C = 37.68 cm

Warm-Up 161
1. r = 5 ft.
2. A = 78.5 sq. ft.
3. C = 31.4 ft.

Warm-Up 162
1. r = 7.5 ft.
2. A = 176.6 sq. ft.
3. C = 47.1 ft.

Warm-Up 163
1. 12.56 cu. in.
2. 2.355 cu. in.
3. Yes, the cylinder holds 18.84 cu. in.

Warm-Up 164
1. 50.24 cu. in.
2. Yes

Warm-Up 165
1. V = 96 cu. ft.
2. V = 165,888 cu. in.
3. V = 48 cu. in.
4. 3,456 bricks
5. Yes

Warm-Up 166
1. V = 120 cu. ft.
2. V = 207,360 cu. in.
3. V = 48 cu. in.
4. 4,320 bricks
5. No

Warm-Up 167
1. V = 360 cu. ft.
2. V = 180 cu. ft.

Warm-Up 168
1. V = 1,152 cu. ft.
2. V = 576 cu. ft.

Warm-Up 169
V = 384 cu. ft.

Warm-Up 170
V = 840 cu. ft.

Warm-Up 171
1. 87 driven early
2. 108 driven late
3. 67 walked/biked
4. 326 total
5. 8 more

Warm-Up 172
1. 47.9% or 48% early
2. 52.1% or 52% late
3. 59.8% or 60% with parents
4. 19.6% or 20% by bus
5. 20.6% or 21% walked/biked

Warm-Up 173
1. corn dogs: 21
2. hot dogs: 27

3. veggie plate: 7
4. brought lunch: 18
5. surveyed: 73

Warm-Up 174
1. 24.7% or 25% brought lunch
2. 28.8% 29% corn dogs
3. 37% hot dogs
4. 9.6% or 10% veggie plate
5. The school cafeteria staff could use this data to choose popular menus.
6. Parents would know when to send lunch based on which lunches are most popular.

Warm-Up 175
1. 47, 49, 53, 57, 59, 61, 79
2. range = 32
3. mode = none
4. median = 57
5. mean = 57.9 or 58

Warm-Up 176
1. 51, 52, 67, 70, 70, 78, 88
2. range = 37
3. mode = 70
4. median = 70
5. mean = 68

Warm-Up 177
1. range = 10
2. mode = 19
3. median = 19
4. mean = 19

Warm-Up 178
1. 17 dimes
2. the mean (average)

Warm-Up 179
1. range = $0.76
2. mode = none
3. median = $0.435 or $0.44
4. mean = $0.5025 or $0.50

Warm-Up 180
1. One would be likely to find about $0.44 to $0.50 because that is the median and mean values students had.
2. The mean is probably the best indicator when the mode and median are relatively close.
3. With an even number of numbers, average the 2 middle numbers to find the median.

Warm-Up 181
1. mode = 35, 40, and 65
2. median = 40
3. mean = 45

Warm-Up 182
40 mph

Warm-Up 183
1st quartile: 36, 40, 40, 44, 44, 56, 60, 64
2nd quartile: 65, 66, 68, 68, 68, 72, 72, 76
3rd quartile: 80, 80, 84, 84, 88, 88, 88, 89
4th quartile: 92, 92, 96, 96, 96, 100, 100, 100

Warm-Up 184
Abigail's score = 2nd quartile
Amanda's score = 3rd quartile

Warm-Up 185
1. 0, 2, 3, 4, 5, 6, 7, 8, 9, 10, 10, 12, 12, 13, 14, 16, 17, 32
2. range = 32
3. mode = 10 and 12
4. median = 9.5
5. mean = 10

Warm-Up 186
1. outlier = 32
2. outliers = 1 and 58

Warm-Up 187
1. Check the line graph for accuracy.
2. The general trend of temperatures was from the low to the high 70s in the first week, and was fairly stable between 70 and 73 the second week.
3. The greatest change of temperature was between Wednesday and Thursday of the first week, 72 to 76 (+ 4 degrees).

Warm-Up 188
1. The general trend of noonday temperatures was downward (decreasing).
2. The change of temperatures went down 18 degrees, from 78 to 60.

Warm-Up 189
1. Gray squirrel
2. River otter
3. range = 28 pounds
4. Jaguarundi and Fisher cat
5. River otter

Warm-Up 190
1. Green anole
2. Banded gecko and Green anole
3. Chuckwalla, Leopard lizard, and Desert iguana
4. Gila monster

ANSWER KEY (cont.)

Warm-Up 191
1. 1 hour
2. 9 hours
3. Caroline
4. Briana = 21 hours
   Caroline = 23 hours
5. watching TV and listening to music

Warm-Up 192
1. 5 hours (3 hours playing an instrument + 2 hours listening to music)
2. Briana talked on the phone for 6 hours total.
3. Caroline cleaned for 1 hour more.
4. Caroline is probably more interested in sports because the graph shows that she spent more time playing sports on the weekend.

Warm-Up 193
1. sports
2. 15 votes
3. music videos and comedy
4. 20 votes

Warm-Up 194
1. music videos and love stories
2. comedy and history
3. news
4. nature/science and history

Warm-Up 195
1. 2 inches
2. 10 inches
3. between weeks 7 and 8, and between weeks 8 and 9
4. during weeks 9 and 10
5. 32 inches

Warm-Up 196
1. week 1
2. week 6
3. 28 inches
4. They both grew fast from the 5th to 9th weeks. They differed in that the corn stopped growing between weeks 9 and 10.

Warm-Up 197
1. 1/6
2. 5/6
3. 1/6
4. 3/6 or 1/2
5. 4/6 or 2/3
6. 3/6 or 1/2

Warm-Up 198
1. 1/5 or 1:5
2. 5/1 or 5:1
3. 3/3 or 3:3
4. 6/0 or 6:0
5. 2/4 or 2:4

Warm-Up 199
1. Results will vary.
2. 8/16 or 1/2
3. Answers will vary.

Warm-Up 200
1. 1/6
2. 2/12 or 1/6
3. 1/6
4. 4/12 or 1/3
5. 0/6

Warm-Up 201
1. 10/400 or 1/40, or 2.5 %
2. 15/400 or 3/80, or 3.75%
3. 25/400 or 1/16, or 6.25%

Warm-Up 202
1. 25/500 or 1/20, or 5%
2. 20/500 or 1/25, or 4%
3. 45/500 or 9/100, or 9%

Warm-Up 203
1. 5/6 x 5/12 = 25/72, or about 34.7%
2. 5/6 x 1/2 = 5/12, or about 41.7%
3. 5/12 x 1/2 x 5/6 = 25/144, or about 17.4%

Warm-Up 204
1. 3/4 x 2/3 = 1/2, or 50%
2. 1/2 x 2/3 = 1/3, or about 33.3%
3. 2/3 x 3/4 x 1/2 = 1/4, or 25%

Warm-Up 205
2/10 x 1/9 = 1/45, or about 2.2%

Warm-Up 206
2/20 x 1/19 = 1/190, or about 0.5%

Warm-Up 207
1. 4/52 or 1/13, or about 7.7%
2. 8/52 or 2/13, or about 15.4%
3. 12/52 or 3/13, or about 23%

Warm-Up 208
1. 4/52 or 1/13, or about 7.7%
2. 4/20 or 1/5, or 20%

Warm-Up 209
2/8 x 1/7 = 1/28, or about 3.6%

Warm-Up 210
1. 3/6 or 1/2, or 50%
2. 3/6 x 2/5 x 1/4 = 1/20, or 5%

Warm-Up 211
1. P = 2(n + x)
2. P = 2(3n) or P = 6n
3. P = 36 in.

Warm-Up 212
1. A = n(x)
2. A = 2n(n) or A = 2n^2
3. A = 72 sq. in.

Warm-Up 213
1. r = 650/5
2. r = 130 yards per minute

Warm-Up 214
1. r = 5,280/20
2. r = 264 feet per minute

Warm-Up 215
$42 + .08($42) + 2 = $47.36

Warm-Up 216
1. g + 0.08g + 4
2. $36 + .08($36) + 4 = $42.88

Warm-Up 217
n = 26, She needs $26 more.

Warm-Up 218
1. n + $35 = $53
2. n = $18, She needs $18 more.

Warm-Up 219
1. 48 ÷ 4 = m
2. m = 12; He received $12.

Warm-Up 220
1. $124 x 4 = t
2. t = 496 tomatoes

Warm-Up 221
Do the work in the parentheses.
Do the work with the exponents.
Multiply and divide in order from left to right.
Add and subtract in order from left to right.

Warm-Up 222
(9 x 8 – 12) ÷ 6 – 4 + 5(5) – 20 + 4
60 ÷ 6 – 4 + 25 – 20 + 4
10 – 4 + 25 – 20 + 4
15
He had 15 cards left.

Warm-Up 223
1. 5 + 3 + (3 x <u>2</u>) + (<u>4</u> x 2)
2. $22

Warm-Up 224
1. [(7 x <u>2</u>) + (4 x <u>6</u>)] ÷ 2 + 4 + 3
2. $26

Warm-Up 225
29 inches

Warm-Up 226
73 inches

Warm-Up 227
(9 x 8 ÷ 12 + 3 x 4 ÷ 12) ÷ 7
(72 ÷ 12 + 12 ÷ 12) ÷ 7
(6 + 1) ÷ 7
7 ÷ 7 = 1
$1

Warm-Up 228
(8 x 12) ÷ 4 x 3 + (4 + 24 + 8)
  ÷ 6 x 8
96 ÷ 4 x 3 + 36 ÷ 6 x 8
24 x 3 + 6 x 8
72 + 48 = 120
$120

Warm-Up 229
1. All products equal 0.
2. Any number times 0 is 0.

Warm-Up 230
1. The number added to 6,578 is 0.
  The number times 6,578 is 1.
2. Any number plus 0 equals the
  number itself. Any number
  times 1 equals the number itself.

Warm-Up 231
1. 1/4 x 4/1 = 1
  2/5 x 5/2 = 1
  1 1/4 x 4/5 = 1
2. Reverse the numerator and
  denominator to get the
  reciprocal. Any number times
  its reciprocal equals 1.

Warm-Up 232
1. -9/5 x -5/9 = 1
  2/7 x 3 1/2 = 2/7 x 7/2 = 1
  3/13 x 13/3 = 1
2. Any number times its reciprocal
  equals 1.

Warm-Up 233
1. Function rule is $y = x(3) + 4$

2.

Value of x	Value of y
3	13
4	16
5	19
6	22
7	25

3. y = 34
4. y = 43

Warm-Up 234
1. Function rule is $y = 3x - 3$

2.

Value of x	Value of y
1	0
2	3
3	6
4	9
5	12
6	15

Warm-Up 235
1. Function rule is $(2x)^2 - 7$

2.

Value of x	Value of y
1	-3
2	9
3	29
4	57
5	93
6	137
7	189

Warm-Up 236
1. Function rule is $x^3 - 3$

2.

Value of x	Value of y
1	-2
2	5
3	24
4	61
5	122
6	213
7	340

Warm-Up 237
1. 28n + 12d + 11q = 535
2. 28n = $1.40
  12d = $1.20
  11q = $2.75
  Total = $5.35

Warm-Up 238
1. 7q + 26d + 14n = x
2. 7q = $1.75
  26d = $2.60
  14n = $0.70
  Total (x) = $5.05

Warm-Up 239
Lauren is 10 years old.

Warm-Up 240
1. 6x + 1 = 43
2. Karen is 7 years old.

Warm-Up 241
1. 7x + 3 = 66
2. Susan is 9 years old.

Warm-Up 242
1. 11x + 2 = 68
2. Lisa is 6 years old.

Warm-Up 243
1.

Marbles (m)	Cost (c)
1	$3.75
2	$7.50
3	$11.25
4	$15.00
5	$18.75
6	$22.50

2. c = $3.75(12) = $45

Warm-Up 244
1. c = 1.75b

2.

Bags (b)	Cost (c)
1	$1.75
2	$3.50
3	$5.25
4	$7.00
5	$8.75
6	$10.50

3. c = $1.75(14) = $24.50

Warm-Up 245
1. Check graph for accuracy.
  Plotted points should be:
  (1, 5)   (4, 11)
  (2, 7)   (5, 13)
  (3, 9)   (6, 15)
2. Yes, the equation produces a
  straight line.

Warm-Up 246
Check graph for accuracy.
Plotted points should be:
(1, 2)   (6, 7)
(2, 3)   (7, 8)
(3, 4)   (8, 9)
(4, 5)   (9, 10)
(5, 6)   (10, 11)

Warm-Up 247
d(15) + d(22) + d(18)
$18.75 + $27.50 + $22.50 =
$68.75
OR
$1.25(55) = $68.25

Warm-Up 248
c(12) + c(9) + c(19)
$23.40 + $17.55 + $37.05 = $78
OR
$1.95(40) = $78

Warm-Up 249
Midpoints:
Pair 1 = 5/8
Pair 2 = 11/16
Pair 3 = 11/12

Warm-Up 250
Midpoints:
Pair 1 = 9.15
Pair 2 = 0.435
Pair 3 = 2.125